Cassell's

Advanced Short Course

Joanna Gray

Cassell

Contents

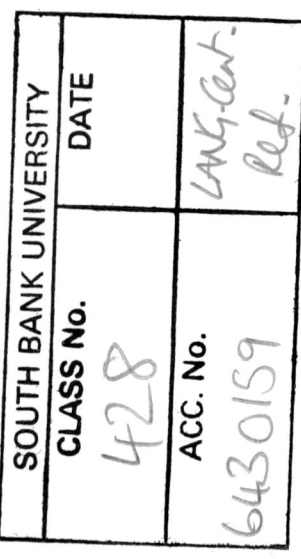

Introduction

To the student

There is an old English saying which claims that 'the more you learn the more you need to learn'. You have probably learnt a great deal about the English language but you may have lacked opportunities to develop productive skills.

Cassell's Advanced Short Course concentrates on the development of skills in speaking, listening, reading and writing, with special emphasis on style and choice of language. In every unit, opportunities are provided for you to express your personal opinions and discuss timely and relevant issues.

A short section is devoted to attitudes in Britain today which provides the basis for interesting comparisons with attitudes in other countries.

You may be using **Cassell's Advanced Short Course** in Britain where you will be able to transfer classroom experiences to daily life situations. If you are studying in another country, you may use, or be preparing to use, English in the context of international communication for study, business or travel.

We hope that this book, with its variety of activities and practice, will encourage and stimulate your interest and fluency in English. And that you will carry on learning.

To the teacher

Cassell's Advanced Short Course is designed to be used by advanced students, for example, those who have reached the standard of post-First Certificate English. It aims to provide opportunities for such students to develop their own communicative skills within a framework of topical and controversial subjects.

The course has no grammatical emphasis. We have assumed that students have acquired a cognitive knowledge of structures and usage. **Cassell's Advanced Short Course** concentrates on transferring and developing cognitive knowledge into communicative skills. You, the teacher, will have to determine:

when, or if, structural, functional or phonological 'errors' interfere with communication;

when and how to monitor, clarify and correct.

The Introduction to each unit sets the scene and states learning objectives. You may want to use the text of the Introduction to test and extend students' lexical and structural usage. Should you later decide to evaluate student learning, the focal points of each unit could be used as a basis for evaluation.

There is a range of listening activities in a variety of situations. In some activities, students are asked to listen for and select specific information. In others, students are encouraged to interpret the attitude of the speaker, the effect on the listeners and the success of the interaction. Reading and writing activities are based on authentic texts, which are informative and challenging. Speaking develops naturally from the stimuli provided by listening, reading and visual elements.

General notes for teachers are provided for each unit. These notes are intended to serve as suggestions rather than teaching plans and the teacher should feel free to ignore them. Above all, **Cassell's Advanced Short Course** attempts to be flexible. Please do not feel that you must begin with Unit 1 and work through systematically. This freedom of choice, together with the open-ended activities, should prove to be productive and stimulating for teacher and students. We hope that you will enjoy using **Cassell's Advanced Short Course.**

1 What do you want to know?

Introduction

Our daily lives are filled with questions: friendly questions, casual questions, official questions, vital questions. The way in which these questions are asked and answered can determine the warmth of the reception you receive, the facilities you are offered, whether permission is given or refused, or even something as vital as the quality of care you receive.

In this unit, the focal points will be the reasons for asking particular questions, the choice of forms of questions, the different intonation patterns of questions and appropriate responses.

1 Listening activity 1

Listen to two people asking questions. You will find a great many differences in the way the questions are asked.

A Analysis
a   Where do you think the questions were asked?
b   Who do you think the questioners were?
c   What was the purpose of the questions?
d   What differences did you hear in the form of the questions?

B Discussion
In pairs, decide:
a   the attitudes of the questioners
b   how the attitudes are indicated by intonation
c   how the form of the answers is related to the form of the questions.

Have you been asked questions, similar to the ones you have just heard, recently? If so, how did you feel about them?

2 Reading activity 1

We not only listen to questions and give spoken answers; we read questions and implied questions in forms and questionnaires. Look at the excerpts from forms on the opposite page. Study the language and decide what the purpose and nature of each form is. The first one is given to you as an example.

A Analysis
a   What words in the questionnaires/forms helped you decide on the subject matter?
b   What differences did you notice in the presentation?

B Discussion
a   What sorts of form do you have to fill in?
b   Are there any forms, or parts of forms, you would refuse to fill in?
c   Do you think forms can become a nuisance? Why/Why not?
d   Which forms are most difficult to answer?

Please complete clearly in BLOCK CAPITALS
Veuillez remplir lisiblement en LETTRES MAJUSCULES
Bitte deutlich in DRÜCKSCHRIFT ausfüllen

Family name
Nom de famille
Familienname

Forenames
Prénoms
Vornamen

Sex
Sexe **(M,F)**
Geschlecht

Date of birth | Day | Month | Year | **Place of birth**
Date de naissance | | | | Lieu de naissance
Geburtsdatum | | | | Geburtsort

Occupation
Profession
Beruf

Nationality
Nationalité
Staatsangehörigkeit

Address in United Kingdom
Adresse en Royaume Uni
Adresse im Vereinigten Königreich

Signature
Signature
Unterschrift

CAT

---

d) Have you had or are you awaiting any medical or surgical investigation or treatment for any disease or serious injury not mentioned above?

e) Have you had a proposal accepted on special terms or declined for either Life or Permanent Health Insurance?

Do you intend to:
a) Reside outside the United Kingdom?

b) Participate in any sport or pastime generally considered to be dangerous, such as competitive motor sports, mountaineering, aviation (other than as a fare paying passenger) or underwater activities?

a) Have you smoked any cigarettes within the last 12 months?
b) Have you any intention of smoking cigarettes in the future?

a)

b)

Please now sign the declaration that follows. If you have dictated your answer I/We, the person(s) proposing to effect the policy, declare that to the best of my complete in every particular, and together with the statement which may be m assured in connection with this proposal, shall be the basis of the contract betw I/We, the life/lives to be assured, declare that to the best of my/our knowledge, complete in every particular. I/We consent to Guardian seeking medical inform me/us concerning anything which affects my/our physical or mental health or s which a proposal has been made for insurance on my life/our lives and I/we au

---

TR079

Before filling in this section please read the n

1. Please indicate your accommodation requirements:

☐ bed and breakfast only
☐ bed, breakfast and evening meal
☐ bed, breakfast and occasional meal

2. All accommodation used by the school is of good quality and has been inspected by the school. The families who live nearest are usually the most expensive, although of course the general facilities offered will influence the price to some extent. We will do all we can to find you a nice family at a good price, but the stronger your preferences the more this restricts the families that are suitable for you: it may mean you have to pay more.

Please indicate here the maximum amount that you want to pay £

3. Please answer the following questions:
a) Would you like a host family with children?
b) Would you like a lot of contact with your host?
c) Do you smoke?
d) Do you have a strong preference for a home without animals?
e) Will you be coming by car?
f) Are you willing to share a room if single rooms are not available?

	Yes	No	Not Important
	☐	☐	☐
	☐	☐	☐
	☐	☐	☐
	☐	☐	☐
	☐	☐	☐
	☐	☐	☐

☐ hotel
maximum price
per night: £

Fees (see dates and f

APPLICANT 1	**APPLICANT 2** To be completed where joint income mortgage is required.
Name	
Address	

Telephone no. **Business** _____ Home _____

_____ Date of Birth _____

Basic Income £ _____ p.a./p.w. £ _____ p.a./p.w.

Overtime/Bonus £ _____ p.a./p.w. £ _____ p.a./p.w.

Deposit Available £ _____

Please let me know, without commitment, how much I could borrow on mortgage on the above income/s and supply a comparison quotation.

OR

Mortgage agreed with _____ of £ _____ over ____ years

Please supply a comparison quotation based on the above mortgage arrangements.

3 Writing activity

This is part of a hospital admission form. You are a patient. Fill in the required information.

MERCY HOSPITAL
Patient Admission Form

Section A This section to be filled in by the patient. Please use BLOCK CAPITALS for questions 1–5.

1 Surname_____

2 Other names_____

3 Nationality_____

4 Address in Britain_____

_____

5 Next of kin (name)_____

For Section B of the form, a nurse asks the patient questions and fills in the information. Write the questions that the nurse will need to ask. Avoid using the words on the form as far as possible.

Section B For official use only

1 Age_____

2 Date of birth_____

3 Allergies_____

4 Medication being taken_____

5 Dietary restrictions_____

6 Patient's reason for admission_____

7 Patient's worries/anxieties_____

A Analysis

a How many of the questions are asking for facts?
b How many are asking for impressions?
c What questions of this type might be asked in an interview for a job?
d Would you ask a friend these questions or similar questions?
e Would you ask a casual acquaintance such questions?

B Discussion

Look at these examples of direct and indirect language:

Direct How old are you?
Indirect Do you remember the Beatles?

Direct What are your problems?
Indirect Something seems to be worrying you.

a How do you feel about the English use of indirect language? Is it polite, or hypocritical?
b Nurses are allowed to ask direct questions because of their role. In what other situations are direct questions expected and acceptable?
c What questions do you dislike being asked? Why?

C Roleplay

Work in pairs. One of you should ask questions. The other should respond, either by answering the question or avoiding giving a direct answer.
   Here are some examples:

Why is your hair so long?
– Because I like long hair.
– What a rude/strange question!

How much do you earn?
– £500 a month.
– I don't really think it's any of your business.

What are your qualifications?
– BSc and MPhil.
– Why do you ask?
– Why do you want to know?

Your hair has really grown, hasn't it?
– Yes, it grows very quickly.

What a beautiful car. You must be doing well.
– Not too badly, thank you.

How did you manage to find such a good job?
– It wasn't so difficult.

4 Reading activity 2

Read the following newspaper article. Pay particular attention to the style and choice of language.

There was an interesting display of temper and inconsistency in the House yesterday. First we heard Mr Jeremy Robbins (Con) defending the rights of the people. Out of character, you might say. But, in this case, the rights referred to were the rights of people to hunt foxes.

In hot pursuit came the impassioned oratory of Mr Tom Jennings (Lib), who seemed to have dedicated his life to the rights of the whale.

The devotion of the two gentlemen might be more impressive were we not faced by urgent decisions affecting the fate of the whole human race.

The speeches took the form of endless questions. It goes without saying that the questions were purely rhetorical. Mr Robbins asked whether the House was aware that the fox was a form of vermin: how many Members had seen a chicken farm wiped out by the attacks of these merciless beasts? He then questioned how they could expect farmers – the backbone of our economy – to survive if predatory animals could not be exterminated.

Mr Jennings's questions were less openly propagandist. He gently queried whether the Honourable Members had any idea of the number of whales slaughtered every year. Were they aware of the greedy, senseless reasons for this butchery? He wondered how they could sleep soundly knowing that a valuable and unique species of mammal was being systematically destroyed.

Both Mr Jennings and Mr Robbins appear to have done some homework. The question is – have they been pursuing the right subjects?

After you have read it, choose the headline you think is most appropriate.

Human or animal rights? **SAVE THE WHALE!**

'Bloody' debate in Commons

Can the whale be saved?

MPs come to verbal blows

A Analysis
a According to the journalist, how many questions were asked?
b What were the questions reported here?
c The two speeches were intended to impress and persuade, so emotive language was used. How many words can you find that refer to killing?
d Work in pairs or small groups to find words or expressions that means the same as:

show   cruel   type   reason
completely   obviously   destroyed

B Discussion
a How do you think the journalist feels about the speakers and their subjects?
b How important do you think it is to preserve endangered species of animals?
c What is your experience of the use of emotive language in the media? How do you feel about this use?

▣ 5 Listening activity 2

Listen to this radio talk. The broadcaster, Patrick
Simmons, mentions several issues involved in
smoking. Some points are listed on the right.

A Analysis
a Listen to what he has to say and make notes
– in your own words – about other points he
makes.

B Discussion
Exchange views and experiences with other
members of the class.
a Are there any places where you think
smoking should be prohibited? If so, why?
b What do you think would happen to the
world's economy if tobacco-growing was
universally abolished?
c What suggestions could you make to people
who would like to stop smoking?

SMOKING

relaxing

smelly

May we remind
patrons that all
auditoria in this
cinema are
NON SMOKING

📼 6 Attitudes in Britain

London Regional Transport has recently decided to ban smoking on the Underground. Regular Tube users have been asked about their reactions to the ban.
You can read their reactions below:

a Diabolical liberty, if you ask me.

b I'm delighted. At last a really positive effort to stop people smoking.

c It's all very well, but who's going to enforce it? Haven't got enough staff as it is.

d We are confident that the public will understand that smoking as a social activity is not being condemned.

e Make my job easier, won't it? All them filthy carriages.

f Thank God for buses!

g There's no way I'm going to travel from Morden to Moorgate without a fag.

h A compromise is the answer. After all, smokers are fare payers, too.

i Don't suppose it bothers them City types. Sloane Square or Hampstead to the Barbican. Luxury homes, expense accounts, big offices and fat cigars when they get there.

j Storm in a teacup. If they really want to do something, what about muggings?

Analysis and discussion

Work in groups of three or four and discuss the attitudes of the speakers. Here are a few descriptive words to help you start.

angry
apathetic
class-conscious
concerned
conciliatory

callous
cynical
disillusioned
uninvolved
honest

All these people were asked the same question. What do you think the question was?
How many of the people who were questioned gave indirect answers? Suggest possible reasons for this.

2 I can speak for myself

Introduction

The word *assertive* has become an important one in social and business contacts. *The Oxford Advanced Learner's Dictionary of Current English* defines assertive in the following way:

> **assertive:** *adj* having or showing positive assurance: *speaking in an* (assertive) *tone.*

But how do we recognise assurance? What is considered to be assertive in one country might be considered as aggressive in another. And we are all aware that aggressive behaviour – real or imagined – can provoke aggression in others.

In this unit the focal points will be assertive and aggressive language and the effects of such language. Forms of agreement and disagreement and some English language conventions will also be studied.

---

1 Listening activity 1

Look at the two menus opposite and decide what the similarities and differences are.

a Why might some people choose one rather than the other?
b Which menu would you choose? Why?

Listen to two people saying what they want to eat. They are both attending the same weekend conference.

A Analysis
a Who were the statements addressed to?
b What differences are there in the form of the statements?
c Which of the speakers is more likely to have interesting meals? Why?

B Discussion
This time listen to the statements and the responses they produce.

Working in pairs, decide:

a the attitudes of the two conference members
b the attitude of the catering manager to the two members
c how you would have reacted to each member if you had been catering manager.

These adjectives may help you describe attitudes:

tolerant	assertive	co-operative
biased	aggressive	warm
constructive	considerate	cold
obstructive	selfish	arrogant

MENU

Black Olives

Asparagus

Eggs in Mushroom Sauce

Avocado and Spinach Soup

Cold Cucumber Soup

Vegetable Curry

Stuffed Peppers

Potato and Onion Pie

MENU

Tomato Soup

•

Egg salad

Cheese salad

Baked potato

Beans on toast

Egg and chips

Beans and chips

Omelette and chips

•

2   Reading activity 1

When reading it is reassuring to be able to answer the following questions:
– Why was this written?
– Why am I reading it?
– Do I really understand it?
– How should I respond?

Look at this advertisement and ask yourself these questions:
– Is this advertisement of any interest to me?
– Is it clear?

REUTERS   REUTERS   REUTERS

Projects Executive

European Marketing

Central London   **£12,000–£13,000**

Reuters, the international news and information organisation, requires an executive in its European Marketing department to manage in detail sectors of the fast-moving data it provides to the international business community. The post is based at its London Head Office.

Continued rapid growth of the Company's Monitor services demands additional management to supervise the scope and content of data in this highly-successful profit-generating area.

He/she will have considerable contact with our sales and marketing staff throughout Europe and elsewhere, and with technical operations staff.

Candidates must be numerate, capable of driving many simultaneous projects

smoothly and achieving deadlines. A degree is essential. Knowledge of the financial markets and project management experience are highly desirable. (Technical knowledge of computer databases is not a particular requirement.)

Career prospects within Reuters are excellent, both within the UK and overseas. The remuneration package includes six weeks holiday, free life assurance, subsidised restaurant and BUPA cover.

For a full job description and an application form, please telephone Mrs K. Boncal, Recruitment Executive, on 01-251 7095, or write to her at:–

REUTERS
85 Fleet Street, London EC4P 4AJ
This position is open to men and women

REUTERS   REUTERS   REUTERS

A   Analysis

What is the key information? There are two examples to help you.

Employer: _Reuters (Int. news, info service)_

Type of job: _Marketing (Projects Exec.)_

Location: _Europe (based London)_

Salary: _____

Requirements: _____

Advantages: _____

Career prospects: _____

Action to take (if any): _____

Which of the following statements is true?

a   Reuters require an executive to manage all business data.
b   Candidates must have organising ability.
c   Male candidates will be given preference.
d   Computer experience would be a distinct advantage.
e   A knowledge of languages would be useful.

B   Discussion

a   How often do you look at job advertisements?
b   Why do you look at them?
c   What would persuade you to look for another job?
d   What would you look for when considering a change of job?

Here is a list of factors considered to be important by a random group of interviewees:

promotion	salary
benefits	increments
security	scope
pension	location
holidays	responsibility
travel	working hours
interest	further training
company car	sports facilities

C Roleplay

Work in pairs. One should take the part of the Personnel Officer responsible for short-listing candidates for a job; the other should be the applicant. Use the question and answer skills practised in Unit 1. The applicant should be assertive, but not aggressive.

3 Writing activity

Either:

a If you find one of these jobs interesting, write a letter asking for an application form, or an appointment.

or:

b Write a letter to an English referee explaining why you have decided not to apply for one of the jobs.

YOUTH AND COMMUNITY SERVICE

Lancashire County Council

AN EQUAL OPPORTUNITIES EMPLOYER

Re-Advertisement

BLACKBURN AND DARWEN DISTRICT YOUTH TEAM

Required for October 22, 1984

SCALE — J.N.C. RANGE 3 (1–5)

DISTRICT YOUTH WORKER

Experienced and qualified Youth Worker for a post which will involve developmental work predominantly with girls from the Asian community. The ability to speak Urdu and/or Gujurati an advantage.

Forms/further details from/to the District Education Officer, Education Office, Town Hall, Blackburn. SAE Please.

Closing date: August 16, 1984.

SOUTH EAST THAMES REGIONAL HEALTH AUTHORITY

CAREERS WITH COMPUTERS

Computers are now used extensively to improve health care in Britain. The provision of computer services is expanding rapidly and skilled, well trained staff are needed to develop the necessary systems.

We can offer the appropriate training to the right candidates for this worthwhile, yet challenging career. No experience is required but the ability to think clearly and reason logically is vital.

Candidates should possess a degree or good 'A' Levels.

The starting salary is £5,728 rising by annual increments to £6,712 per annum (increase pending).

To obtain an application form, write to:
Regional Systems Development Officer, London SE11 4TH.

PERSONAL ASSISTANT/SECRETARY

required for Chief Executive of a new Company involved in film and television industry.

Requirements include:
- Ability and initiative to work on your own and to develop the position to its full potential.
- Good administrative and secretarial skills.
- Experience in the film and television industry would be useful, but not essential.

Good salary, negotiable according to age and experience.

Please reply with typed c.v. to:

Mrs. Clare Dibble
32 Eccleston Square, London SW1V 1PB
Tel. 01-834 2300

4   Reading activity 2

No title or source is given for the reading passage opposite.
However, it is clearly written and, when you have analysed and
discussed it, you will probably be able to guess the origin.

A   Analysis

a   What are the main points and arguments?
Express them in your own words.

b   What do you think the aims of the writer(s)
were:
– to sell   – to inform   – to teach?

c   Find examples of assertive expressions.

B   Discussion

Working in groups, determine:
a   when the passage might have been written
b   whether the passage is relevant today
c   what the origin of the passage is.

5   Listening activity 2

Listen to this conversation. Here are some questions which will help
you to listen and understand. Read the questions; listen to the tape;
think; listen to the tape again; answer the questions.

A   Analysis

a   The woman said: 'It's not good enough!'
Was she:
1 explaining   2 complaining
3 commenting   4 comparing?

b   The man said: 'Oh, come on, Helen.'
Was he:
1 encouraging   2 dismissive
3 suggesting   4 offering?

c   The man said: 'It's not the end of the world.'
Was he being:
1 helpful   2 optimistic
3 encouraging   4 dismissive?

d   The woman said: 'Why don't you answer
your own question?'
Was she:
1 asking for information   2 suggesting
3 accusing   4 inviting?

e   The man said: 'This isn't getting us anywhere.'
Was he:
1 commenting   2 complaining
3 suggesting action   4 accusing?

Use your own words to complete these
statements.
f   When the woman arrived at the flat she was
feeling . . .
g   The man reacted by . . .
h   The woman responded by . . .
i   Aggression began to change to assertion
when . . .
j   The outcome of the discussion was . . .

B   Discussion
How do you feel about the sort of working
arrangement the couple were discussing?
If you were giving advice based on your
experience, what advice would you give?

WHEN in the Course of human events, it becomes necessary for one people to dissolve the political bands which have connected them with another, and to assume among the powers of the earth, the separate and equal station to which the Laws of Nature and of Nature's God entitle them, a decent respect to the opinions of mankind requires that they should declare the causes which impel them to the separation.—We hold these truths to be self-evident, that all men are created equal, that they are endowed by their Creator with certain unalienable Rights, that among these are Life, Liberty and the pursuit of Happiness.—That to secure these rights, Governments are instituted among Men, deriving their just powers from the consent of the governed.—That whenever any Form of Government becomes destructive of these ends, it is the Right of the People to alter or to abolish it, and to institute new Government, laying its foundation on such principles and organizing its powers in such form, as to them shall seem most likely to effect their Safety and Happiness. Prudence, indeed, will dictate that Governments long established should not be changed for light and transient causes; and accordingly all experience hath shewn, that mankind are more disposed to suffer, while evils are sufferable, than to right themselves by abolishing the forms to which they are accustomed. But when a long train of abuses and usurpations, pursuing invariably the same Object evinces a design to reduce them under absolute Despotism, it is their right, it is their duty, to throw off such government, and to provide new Guards for their future security. —Such has been the patient sufferance of these Colonies; and such is now the necessity which constrains them to alter their former Systems of Government. The history of the present King of Great Britain is a history of repeated injuries and usurpations, all having in direct object the establishment of absolute Tyranny over these States. To prove this, let Facts be submitted to a candid world.—He has refused his Assent to Laws, the most wholesome and necessary for the public good.—He has forbidden his Governors to pass Laws of immediate and pressing importance, unless suspended in their operation till his Assent should be obtained; and when so suspended, he has utterly neglected to attend to them.—He has refused to pass other Laws for the accommodation of large districts of people, unless those people would relinquish the right of Representation in the Legislature, a right inestimable to them and formidable to tyrants only.—He has called together legislative bodies at places unusual, uncomfortable, and distant from the depository of their public Records, for the sole purpose of fatiguing them into compliance with his measures.—He has dissolved Representative Houses repeatedly, for opposing with manly firmness his invasions on the rights of the people. —He has refused for a long time, after such dissolutions, to cause others to be elected; whereby the Legislative powers, incapable of Annihilation, have returned to the People at large for their exercise; the State remaining in the meantime exposed to all the dangers of invasion from without, and convulsions from within.—He has endeavoured to prevent the population of these States; for that purpose obstructing the Laws for Naturalization of Foreigners; refusing to pass others to encourage their migrations hither, and raising the conditions of new Appropriations of Lands.—He has obstructed the Administration of Justice, by refusing his Assent to Laws for establishing Judiciary powers.—He has made Judges dependent on his Will alone, for the tenure of their offices, and the amount and payment of their salaries.—He has erected a multitude of New Offices, and sent hither swarms of Officers to harass our people, and eat out their substance. He has kept among us, in times of peace, Standing Armies without the Consent of our legislatures. —He has affected to render the Military independent of and superior to the Civil power.—He has combined with others to subject us to a jurisdiction foreign to our constitution, and unacknowledged by our laws; giving his Assent to their Acts of pretended Legislation:—For quartering large bodies of armed troops among us:—For protecting them, by a mock Trial, from punishment for any Murders which they should commit on the Inhabitants of these States:—For cutting off our Trade with all parts of the world:—For imposing Taxes on us without our Consent:—For depriving us in many cases, of the benefits of Trial by Jury:—For transporting us beyond Seas to be tried for pretended offences:—For abolishing the free System of English Laws in a neighbouring Province, establishing therein an Arbitrary government, and enlarging its Boundaries so as to render it at once an example and fit instrument for introducing the same absolute rule into these Colonies:—For taking away our Charters, abolishing our most valuable Laws and altering fundamentally the Forms of our Governments: —For suspending our own Legislatures, and declaring themselves invested with power to legislate for us in all cases whatsoever.—He has abdicated Government here, by declaring us out of his Protection and waging War against us.—He has plundered our seas, ravaged our Coasts, burnt our towns, and destroyed the lives of our people.—He is at this time transporting large Armies of foreign Mercenaries to compleat the works of death, desolation and tyranny, already begun with circumstances of Cruelty & perfidy scarcely paralleled in the most barbarous ages, and totally unworthy the Head of a civilized nation.—He has constrained our fellow Citizens taken Captive on the High Seas to bear Arms against their Country, to become the executioners of their friends and Brethren, or to fall themselves by their Hands.—He has excited domestic insurrections amongst us, and has endeavoured to bring on the inhabitants of our frontiers, the merciless Indian Savages, whose known rule of warfare, is an undistinguished destruction of all ages, sexes and conditions. In every stage of these Oppressions We have Petitioned for Redress in the most humble terms: Our repeated Petitions have been answered only by repeated injury. A Prince, whose character is thus marked by every act which may define a Tyrant, is unfit to be the ruler of a free people. Nor have We been wanting in attentions to our British brethren. We have warned them from time to time of attempts by their legislature to extend an unwarrantable jurisdiction over us. We have reminded them of the circumstances of our emigration and settlement here. We have appealed to their native justice and magnanimity, and we have conjured them by the ties of our common kindred to disavow these usurpations, which would inevitably interrupt our connections and correspondence. They too have been born deaf to the voice of justice and of consanguinity. We must, therefore, acquiesce in the necessity, which denounces our Separation, and hold them, as we hold the rest of mankind, Enemies in War, in Peace Friends.—

WE, THEREFORE, the Representatives of the UNITED STATES OF AMERICA, in General Congress, Assembled, appealing to the Supreme Judge of the world for the rectitude of our intentions, do, in the Name, and by Authority of the good People of these Colonies, solemnly publish and declare, That these United Colonies are, and of Right out to be FREE AND INDEPENDENT STATES; that they are Absolved from all Allegiance to the British Crown, and that all political connection between them and the State of Great Britain, is and ought to be totally dissolved; and that as Free and Independent States, they have full Power to levy War, conclude Peace, contract Alliances, establish Commerce, and to do all other Acts and Things which Independent States may of right do. —And for the support of this Declaration, with a firm reliance on the protection of divine Providence, we mutually pledge to each other our Lives, our Fortunes and our sacred Honour.

📼 6 Attitudes in Britain

Questions about the 'caring services' in a welfare state provoke a
variety of responses from the public. Among the carers are nurses,
teachers and social workers. Here is a cross-section of responses to
a public opinion poll.

a They're angels. Angels of mercy.

b Look at the holidays they have. I could do with a summer off.

c Interfering lot. Ask a lot of nosey questions.

d When my mum was in, they didn't give *her* much attention.

e They're a gang of lefties, if you ask me.

f What would we do without them?

g However do they cope? I can't manage my own three!

h I wouldn't fancy that kind of work. Takes too much out of you.

i If they can't teach the three Rs, who needs them?

j They're educated, aren't they? They know all about the law and benefits.

k Overworked and underpaid. That's what I reckon.

l I do feel sorry for those young girls. Just imagine the sights they must see.

Analysis and discussion

a Work in groups and decide which comments
   referred to:
   – nurses   – teachers
   – social workers   – all of these

b What questions were asked to prompt these
   responses?

c How many of the speakers seemed to be:
   appreciative   envious
   understanding   uninterested
   suspicious   aggressive
   assertive   resentful?

3 I see what you mean

Introduction

Mutual understanding is basic to communication, and listening is a vital component of understanding. Just hearing is not enough because it is passive. Listening, however, is active, and often involves all the senses.

Effective listening is a skill which can be developed. Good listeners need to develop the ability to separate the relevant from the irrelevant. What is relevant in one situation may be irrelevant in another, and vice versa.

In this unit you will have opportunities to practise listening for facts and details, interpreting attitudes and implied meaning and listening for overall understanding.

---

1 Listening activity 1

Listen to extracts of two telephone conversations and then discuss:

a what the subject of each conversation is
b what the problems are
c whether each conversation is friendly or unfriendly
d what clues have led you to your opinions.

2 Reading activity 1

Below and on page 18, you can see three examples of incomplete or 'telegraphic' communications. With each example, discuss:

a who the message is designed for
b the purpose of the message.

Supply the missing words and information.

SE23 Non Smk; prof pers to share comf. home. Gdn; CH; close BR £45 pw excl. Reply Box 242

POSTCARD

Hope No 8 + plants & cat are OK. Do the same for you in Sept. Channel p. rough / Chalet v. good. Beach clean but crowded. Can't complain. See you Sat.
Love, F, G, P & J

All at No 6 Holmwood
Wychwood
nr Guildford
Surrey
UK

```
URGENT
------

YF 9414 JORD HOSP PROJ

AAA MANY THKS FOR YR INFO ABOUT MR BOB JONES'S VISIT
AMMAN 20 DEC.  KINDLY ADVISE WHICH HOTEL HE STAYING
ENABLE ME CONTACT HIM.


BBB PLS ADVS BJ PHONE NO MY OFFICE AMMAN.

CCC THNKS.

REGARDS NB
= 07091723
```

3   Writing activity

When selecting language for writing, one of the criteria is the degree
of formality or informality appropriate to the context.
Compare and contrast the letters on this page and the next, then
choose the words most
appropriate for each.

a

1 ratify	2 discussions
confirm	chats
OK	discourse

3 lot	4 envoys
conclave	delegates
assembly	chaps

b

1 gratified	2 flat
overjoyed	domicile
happy	residence

3 appropriate	4 view
just right	see
adequate	have sight of

D L S Squires
Managing Director
Squire & Biggs Ltd
Industry House
Liverpool   1 Jan 1981

Dear Mr Squires,

I am writing to 1_____ our previous 2_____
with regard to the coming convention. You will be
addressing the entire 3_____ of approximately
250 international 4_____ . Accommodation and
travel arrangements will have been made and details
will be sent to you well in advance.

We look forward to seeing you then.
Yours sincerely,

G H Hall

Dear old Susie

About time we heard from you, isn't it?
Must be at least 6 months. Seamus has
been suggesting that you'd emigrated.
Seriously, we were 1 _____ to get
your letter.
What good news about the new
2 _____ ! It sounds 3 _____ for
the two of you. Please let us know when we
can 4 _____ it.
Love from all of us, Helen

4   Reading activity 2

It is often necessary to convert written comments and instructions
into spoken language. When this occurs, there are several decisions
to be made and acted upon:
– What is the real message?
– Who is it for?
– How can it best be expressed?

PASSAGE 1
Read this passage carefully and use your analytical and language
skills to do the roleplay that follows.

Advice on safety

When children are being carried in the car, it is the parents' responsibility to make sure that proper safety
precautions are observed.

- Before shutting a door, look out for fingers
  which might be in the opening.

- Children under ten should always ride in the
  back of the car.

- Never leave a child alone in the car.

- Children should never travel on the knee of a
  front seat passenger because of the danger of
  being thrown against the dashboard or
  windscreen in a collision.

- Provision for amusement and diversion should
  be made. A bored and active child can be a
  danger to the driver.

- Avoid travelling long distances on your own with
  a young child.

- Make sure that young children are *not* standing
  between the front and back seats. They could
  be badly bruised in the event of a sudden
  braking.

Roleplay
Work in pairs

Student A
You are planning to visit your parents who live 400 miles away. They are insisting that you should bring your niece. You are worried about driving on your own with a three-year-old child.

Fortunately, you have a friend who is an expert in such matters. Ask for advice.

Student B
You are a safety expert, specialising in children and traffic accidents. Your friend is seeking advice. Can you help?

PASSAGE 2
Read this passage and then discuss the needs and anxieties of the letter writer, and how to pass these on to the hospital authorities.

> Dear Doctor
>   1 Dont no if your the one i should write to but i have to,
>   My husband George Thompson is ill, I did not say much before now George is really ill, aboute three months he is been like it and the hospital doesent do anything for him, another thing in that place they call him George but he dos not arnser to George he's name is Gus, i think i should take him home Doctor they say it is up to you Doctor
>   Please can you help me
>
>   All the best
>   Flora Thompson

5   Listening activity 2

Our own backgrounds, experiences and attitudes influence our interpretation of what we see and hear.

For example:

Statement   Mr Jones works long hours.
Question   How many hours does Mr Jones work?
Answer   There is no 'correct' answer. The answer could be eight or 12, or even 14 hours a day.

What do you consider to be a long working day?

Listen to this description of Mrs Addlestone and answer the questions about her as quickly as possible, based on your first impressions. There will be a time limit. Don't repeat the words used in the description: give precise answers of your own.

a   How old was Mrs Addlestone?
b   How many children had she had?
c   How tall was she?
d   Approximately how much did she weigh?
e   How many cigarettes did she smoke on average?
f   What was her driving like?
g   What time did she usually get up?

A   Analysis
Compare your answers with those of other students.
a   What are the differences?
b   Why do you think they differ?

B   Discussion
a   What effect does the use of ambiguous words have on attitudes and behaviour?
b   Give further examples of such words. How can you clarify the meaning of an ambiguous statement so that everyone interprets it in the same way?

🔊 6 Attitudes in Britain

Britain's tourism industry headed for record earnings in 1984. The forecasts from the British Tourist Authority suggested that there would be more than 13 million visitors and that they would spend £5 billion. The BTA believes that more than 1.2 million people in Britain now depend directly or indirectly on tourism for their livelihood.

Here are selected comments from tourists and residents about their experiences:

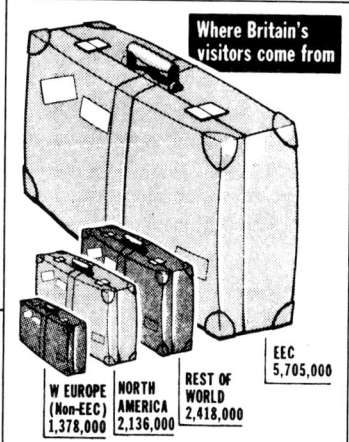

Where Britain's visitors come from

| W EUROPE (Non-EEC) 1,378,000 | NORTH AMERICA 2,136,000 | REST OF WORLD 2,418,000 | EEC 5,705,000 |

a Why don't you call things what they are? There's no circus at Piccadilly.

b I shouldn't come to Brighton in the summer, dear. It's full of them.

c I saw it on Broadway, but the tickets were twice the price.

d Your Underground is good, but not clean . . . and not cheap.

e Where is the fog . . . the Sherlock Holmes fog?

f In my country we studied many English books and I was looking forward to an English breakfast and afternoon tea. I learned that they were important. Where can I find such things?

g Let's get off the motorway. Full of tourist coaches, and no country pubs.

h I refuse to queue for an exhibition when the queue is so disorganised.

i No one told me it would be so green. So many shades of green.

j What is a public convenience?

Analysis and discussion

a Decide who made each comment – a tourist or local resident? What makes you think this?

b Where do you think most of the tourists come from?

c How many of the tourists are surprised by what they have experienced? What did they expect?

d What is your experience of the difference between expectations and reality?

4 Am I making myself clear?

Introduction

Sending messages, written or spoken, is quite a complicated procedure. The person sending the message must:

— know who is to receive the message
— know the purpose of the message
— find an appropriate way of transmitting the message.

Often s/he must also check that the message has been received and interpreted correctly.

This unit will give you practice in recognising, organising and structuring messages; choosing language appropriate to the recipient; and checking that the message sent is the one received.

Visual messages are used internationally to give instructions, warnings, advice and information.

On your own, study the visual messages below and compare your interpretations with those of fellow students.

1 Listening activity 1

Listen to two people giving instructions. Notice the differences in the way the instructions are given.

A Analysis

a   Who was the first speaker talking to?
b   Why were the instructions being given?
c   What was the recipient expected to do?

d   Who do you think the second speaker was speaking to?
e   What was the subject of the instructions?
f   What were the recipients expected to do?

g   Which of the two speakers was easier to follow?
h   Why?

CERTIFICATION TRADE MARK

B Discussion

Listen to the first speaker again. Rearrange the instructions in logical order. Compare your rearrangement with that of a fellow student.

You may find it useful to talk about:
a   the situations when instructions are given
b   the situations when instructions are asked for
c   the language used in these situations.

22

2 Reading activity 1

A Analysis

a What is the subject of the information?

b What is the objective of the leaflet?

c What must the reader be or do?

d What advantages can the reader expect?

e What may the reader do?

f What might the bank do?

g What does the bank promise to do?

B Discussion

a Why can instructions be difficult to follow?

b What do you do when you can't understand written instructions?

c What do you do when you can't follow spoken instructions?

d Give an example from your own experience of a written or spoken instruction you misunderstood. What was the result?

C Roleplay

Choose another student to work with. One of you will give instructions and the other will follow them. Here are some suggestions.

How to:
– sew on a button
– cure hiccups
– apply a plaster
– draw a right-angled triangle
– do push ups.

Now change roles and repeat. If things go wrong, discuss possible reasons.

Saver Plus Account Terms and Conditions

1. You will be bound by these Terms and Conditions when you receive your Saver Plus Card from us.

2. You must be 16 or over to have a Saver Plus Account; the Account is not available for business use.

3. You must maintain a minimum balance of £100. If, and during any period when, the balance of the Account falls below £100, we may pay interest at the Deposit Rate, instead of exercising our rights under Condition 11.

4. You will receive interest at the appropriate Saver Plus Rate. The Rate will be published in our branches and may be varied. Interest rate differentials, the linking of these to Deposit Rate and balance bands may also be varied.

5. Interest is paid in March, June, September and December and calculated on a daily basis on cleared balances.

6. (a) The Card is our property and must be surrendered on request. We may also suspend its use.

(b) The Card is for your use alone. You must keep the personal number secret and take all reasonable care to ensure that the Card is not lost, mislaid or stolen.

(c) If your Card is lost or stolen, you must notify the issuing branch immediately; similarly if you find it again after notifying us of loss or theft.

(d) All Card transactions will be debited to your Account. Note that this is so, despite notification under 6(c) above, if you have failed to comply with 6(b).

7. You may use your Card to draw cash up to £100 per week; and you can withdraw any amount over the counter from the account-holding branch.

8. Any transfers between the Account and your Current Account using the Saver Plus Card must not exceed £9,999, and must be in whole pounds. Transfers will be made the same working day or as soon as possible after this, providing sufficient cleared funds are available.

9. You must not use your Card to overdraw your Account. If your Account becomes overdrawn, monies held in other accounts in your name may be used to pay off the overdraft. Joint account-holders are jointly and severally liable.

10. We will operate the Account unless strikes, interruption of power supplies, machinery failures or causes beyond our control prevent us from doing so.

11. If you do not abide by these Terms and Conditions we may demand return of the Saver Plus Card, close the Account, or convert to a Deposit Account.

12. These Terms and Conditions may be amended by notice in our branches or in the National Press.

3   Writing activity

Give written instructions for one of these situations.
What should a foreign tourist in your country do if he or she:

a   becomes ill
b   wants to hire a car
c   wants to change a plane reservation

d   is a vegetarian
e   would like to thank local people for their hospitality?

4   Reading activity 2

Instructions carry a very direct message. Sometimes, though, our familiarity with certain kinds or patterns of language enables us to convey messages in a less direct way. The language itself is a part of the message's meaning. For example, all cultures have their proverbs and wise sayings. Very often, we quote these without even thinking about their literal meaning because we know so well what point they are meant to convey.

   Look at the four illustrations of well-known English proverbs. What message do you think the drawings give? Compare your interpretations with those of others.

Familiarity with a particular pattern of language means that when it is used we have certain expectations about the message it will convey. So, for example, you may think, when you read the beginning of this passage, that you know what sort of story it is going to be. But you may find, as you read on, that parts of the story are expressed in a strange or inappropriate way.

Once upon a time, great good fortune was showered upon a royal family. The King and Queen were blessed with a daughter. Galia, for that is the name the infant girl was given, was perfect in every way. Her beauty and charm were surpassed only by her intelligence and loving nature. The Princess flourished and was universally adored.

Then, at a stroke, disaster struck the loving family. Galia disappeared. Imagine her distraught mother! Consider her distracted father! And the disturbed populace!

Local residents were shocked by the headlines in their papers. THE COMET: **Tragedy in Local Family.** THE ADVERTISER: **Mysterious Disappearance of Village Favourite.** THE REVIEW: **Our Galia's Gone.**

The mayor and local council called an emergency meeting. For the first time in history, personal interest and politics were forgotten. There was a unanimous decision to offer a handsome reward for information leading to the return of the missing girl.

While the public uproar was at its height and the desolate parents were nursing their grief, Galia was trying to survive. To her surprise, shopkeepers expected her to give them money. Before she travelled on an exceedingly uncomfortable and noisy train, she was expected to produce a small scrap of paper called a ticket. When she smiled at people, they turned away. Not one of them bowed or presented her with flowers. There was one consolation: her friend, Alicia. Alicia brought her apples and told her about the most important thing in the world – jobs!

Galia began her search for a job . . . any job. She went to interview after interview, but wherever she went she was asked about 'qualifications', 'previous experience'. Her answers seemed to confuse the interviewing panels. One rather aggressive lady even told her that 15 years as a princess was hardly a recommendation for a catering job.

Finally, Galia decided that enough was enough. She had a heart-to-heart talk with Alicia and decided to . . .

A Analysis

a What, in particular, reminds you of stories you may have heard when you were a child?

b Identify the parts of the story which are incongruous or odd. Are they incongruous because of the subject matter or the language or both?

c The story has no conclusion. Provide a conclusion which seems appropriate to you.

B Discussion

a Working with other students, compare your conclusions. What relevance does the story have to modern life?

b What experiences have you had that could be comparable to Galia's?

c Compare your thoughts about the messages of the proverbs in the pictures with other people's. Are there any differences? If so, why do you think these occurred?

⟦🔊⟧ 5   Listening activity 2

You are about to hear a recording of the introduction to an unusual
concert. First, listen to the recording. Makes notes of the main
points. Then complete the unfinished statements. Finally, listen to
the recording again and compare your answers.

Here are the statements:

a   The concert is somewhat unusual
because . . .

b   The first work to be heard was composed
by . . .

c   Holmes seems to have been interested
in . . . musical instruments.

d   Holmes' family . . .

e   Holmes is now grateful that . . .

f   The orchestra members have been very
tolerant because . . .

⟦🔊⟧ 6   Attitudes in Britain

The British are proud of their television. There are four main
channels to choose from, two run by the British Broadcasting
Corporation and two by commercial companies. There are no
advertisements on BBC, which gets a large percentage of its
revenue from the licence fee all television owners are obliged to
purchase each year – regardless of whether or not they ever watch
BBC channels! ITV companies and Channel 4 raise most of their
revenue from advertising. Opposite are some comments from TV
viewers:

a I do like the adverts. Have you seen the one about the bloke who drinks that new kind of beer?

b Bad influence on the children.

c Find I'm getting lazy. Easier to sit down than to do something, isn't it?

d Don't like the summer programmes. Nothing but a load of American bought-in rubbish.

e Now it's autumn we'll have football all the weekend. All right for them that likes football.

f Don't know what I'd do without it. A real contact with the world.

g Reckon it's a nice way to escape. What I mean there's so much trouble about, you don't want to know, do you?

h Our committee have decided to recommend to parents that only selective television viewing should be allowed to school-age children.

i Television news often gives a distorted picture of violence. We see the action but not the aftermath.

j Television is the teacher of the future.

k When my Joe said there was a party political broadcast, I told him to switch off. Bad enough listening to them without having to look at them.

l Lots of us condemn it but the last thing to go is always the telly. I wonder why.

Analysis and discussion

a If you were conducting an opinion poll, how would you rate television as a medium of information? Base your conclusions on the comments you have read and heard.

b How do you personally use television? As a convenience, a piece of furniture, a narcotic, entertainment, education?

c Can television give instruction and education? If you believe it can, give some specific examples.

d Has television become a necessity?

5 What should I do?

Introduction

We all have times when we need reassurance, when we turn to someone for information, advice and counsel. The language used in such situations is very important. The person seeking reassurance must be able to explain what the difficulty is – 'get the message across'; the listener must respond appropriately and sensitively. People can find it difficult to choose appropriate language when, as is often the case, they are under stress. If the two people involved are of different linguistic and cultural backgrounds, then problems can arise. Advanced students of English often have to cope with situations which many a native speaker would find difficult to handle.

In this unit there will be opportunities to observe and practise ways of seeking and giving reassurance in a variety of situations.

---

1 Listening activity 1

Before you listen to the tape, study the photographs and discuss:

a where the photographs were taken
b why people would be there
c what sort of information or advice they might need.

Maternity dept.

Out-patients dept.

Intensive therapy unit

Now listen to parts of three telephone conversations. Notice the differences in the reasons for the calls and the ways the callers respond.

A Analysis

a What were the differences in the reasons for the three telephone calls?

b What were the similarities?

c How satisfactory were the telephone calls?

B Discussion

How many of the callers were native speakers of English?

If you had been the caller:

– how would you have dealt with the responses?

– what further information would you have needed?

– what action would you have taken at the end of the telephone conversations?

2   Reading activity 1

People often write to 'agony aunts' in newspapers or magazines if they need advice. Here are three letters which illustrate the types of problem often discussed in print.

A Analysis

a Can you determine the sex of the three writers? Would it make any difference in the advice you gave? If so, how?

b Identify the problems stated in each of the letters. What key words led you to your decision?

B Discussion

When giving advice, we often use verbs such as: must — should — ought to — can — may — could — might — have to. The choice of verbs can determine the urgency and effectiveness of the message. Working in small groups, decide how you would reply if you were Hester. Compare your 'replies' with those of other groups.

Help from Hester

Dear Hester   1

Older people say that you are too young to be in love at 16. Do you think that is true? My English teacher is 26 – unmarried – and I really believe I love him. He smiles at me in class all the time and he likes the things I write. The trouble is that my friends are jealous and they make fun of me. Should I tell him and them how I feel? YOUNG LOVER

Dear Hester   2

I am doing something I would never have thought possible – washing my dirty linen in public. My wife, if she had not left me, would have had something to say. Or, she might have laughed at me. I know I am far too old to be writing to you. I am 56 . . . and homeless. I have a roof over my head, but it is not a home. The children have grown up and lead their own lives. The fact is, I have no-one to turn to. Can you help? MIDDLE-AGED MESS

Dear Hester   3

How would you feel if you were out of a job and had no prospects? I don't want to see my former friends because they look the other way or offer to lend me money. I know that they are embarrassed but so am I. I could do with the money, by the way. I have always been used to a routine and now there is no reason to do anything. I sleep far too much and seldom know what time it is. Can you do anything for me? HOPELESS

3 Writing activity

Some of the major differences between writing and speaking are:

Writing	Speaking
fixed	flexible
no immediate feedback	chance of immediate feedback
no non-verbal clues	chance of non-verbal clues

a Suggest other differences that occur to you and discuss the implications for writing rather than speaking.

b Now complete a letter to a young friend who will have to study English this year. Your friend seems to resent this.

Dear _____,

Your last letter sounded very _____ and _____.

I can understand _____

_____

A few years ago, I _____

_____

and I _____

_____

_____

4 Reading activity 2

A Analysis

a Who do you think the article opposite was written for? What sort of student does the writer of the article advise to consider taking A-level courses?

b List the advantages of staying on to do A-levels. State, in your own words, what specific advice the writer gives.

B Discussion

Secondary education in Britain is, and has been for some time, a subject of furious argument.
– Industrialists claim that not enough attention is paid to technical, scientific and engineering subjects.
– Educationists insist that pupils and students should be given a free choice and that their opportunities in education or employment should not be a political football.
– Parents demand proof that their children are benefiting from education – demands often based on their own experience of school.

a At what age, or stage, do you think young people are capable of making decisions about their future?

If you have made such a decision:

b When did you decide?

c What influences helped you reach your decision?

d What advice would you give to a young friend who had to make such a decision?

A-Levels or Not?

If you are doing reasonably well at school now, you will probably be considering staying on to study for A-levels. The choices made at this stage can have major consequences later, so it is well worth taking time and trouble over them. What factors must you think about?

Firstly, is the A-level route the right one for you? With a few exceptions, A-level courses are academic and do not train you directly for any specific job. They are very taxing – you have to:

– understand basic principles and theory
– be able to analyse and comment on what you study
– be happy to work very intensively
– do a lot of reading and essay writing.

Further, competition for places on degree courses means you need better and better grades to get in. If you fail to achieve the necessary grades, your chances of getting a job with training are not good either, because employers, too, want people with good A-level grades. So if it looks as if you might have problems getting good grades, or are practical – rather than academically-minded – or you want to start training for work as soon as possible, then look at alternative courses that your school or local Further Education College can offer, or training courses with O-level entry. This does mean, though, that you may be restricting the range of careers open to you.

Should you decide to follow the A-level path, statistics and career advisors have some pointers for you. You may be tempted to choose the easy option – the subjects that you have already studied and find easy. It is more important to consider what really interests you. Then you will be better able to cope with the difficult and boring parts of the course.

Finally, find out as much as you can about the subjects you are thinking of studying. Do not assume you will like A-level History or Physics just because you are enjoying the O-level course in that subject.

5 Listening activity 2

Read the questions below. Then listen to an example of someone talking about giving information, advice and counsel.
Finally, answer the questions.

a Why can Mary Gerard sympathise with the elderly person at home?

b What does Mary imply are the special dangers for the elderly at home?

c What misconception about where the elderly live does Mary mention?

d What might have happened on one occasion if Mary Gerard hadn't visited Mrs Collins?

e What can neighbours of elderly people learn from Mary's story?

f What advice and counsel, based on Mary's story, would you give to anyone looking after elderly people living alone?

🔊 6 Attitudes in Britain

Seeking advice from the stars, or palmists, or fortune-tellers is not peculiar to the British. In many countries there are people who determine their actions and attitudes according to their horoscopes or who secretly consult some occult source of counsel.

Others refuse to believe that these sources have any influence on their lives.

Visitors to Britain are sometimes surprised, however, at how often horoscopes are mentioned, and astonished at the range of people interested in discussing them.

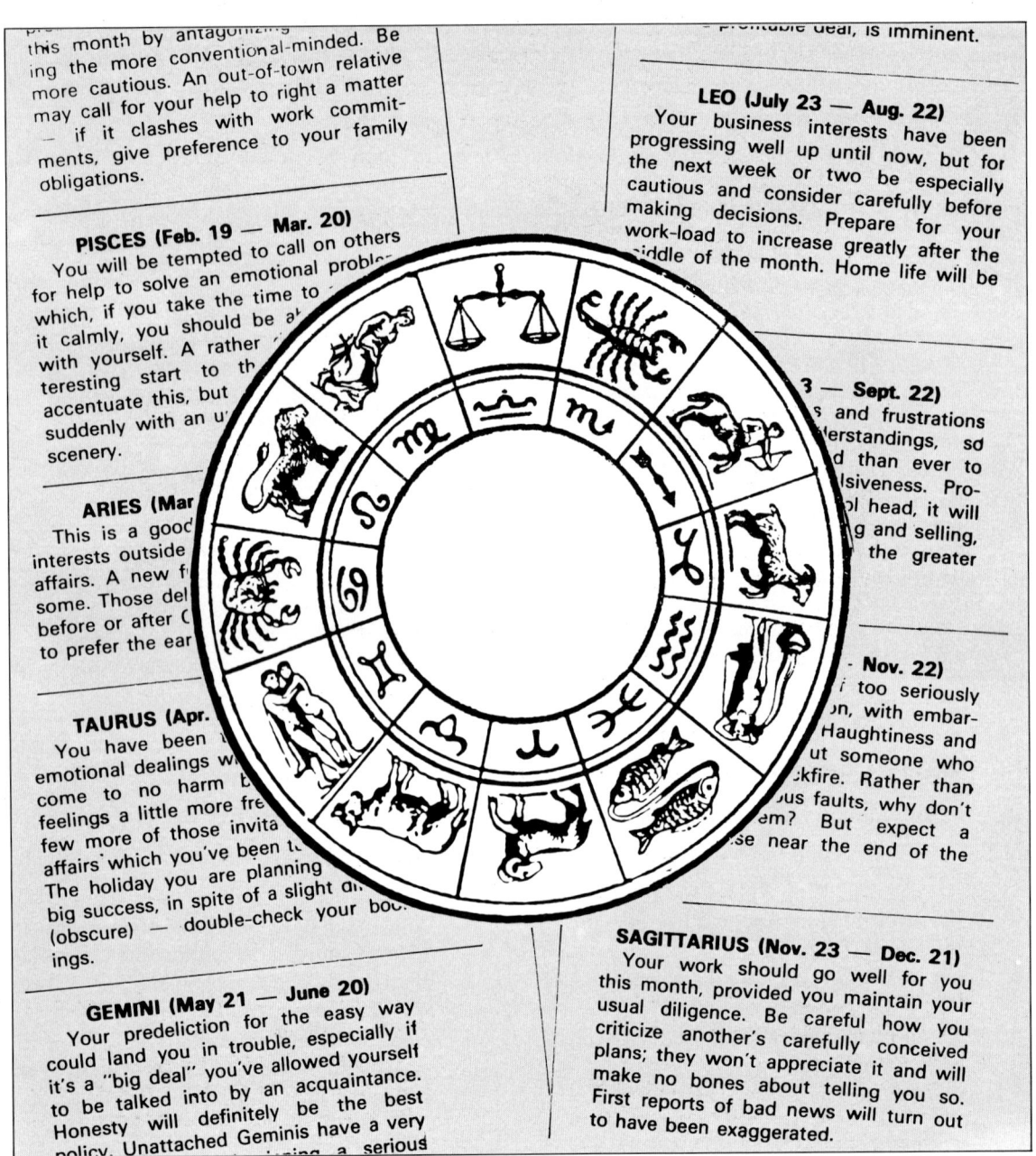

this month by antagonizing the more conventional-minded. Be more cautious. An out-of-town relative may call for your help to right a matter — if it clashes with work commitments, give preference to your family obligations.

PISCES (Feb. 19 — Mar. 20)
You will be tempted to call on others for help to solve an emotional probl... which, if you take the time to ... it calmly, you should be a... with yourself. A rather ... teresting start to th... accentuate this, but ... suddenly with an u... scenery.

ARIES (Mar...
This is a good ... interests outside ... affairs. A new f... some. Those del... before or after C... to prefer the ear...

TAURUS (Apr...
You have been ... emotional dealings w... come to no harm b... feelings a little more fre... few more of those invita... affairs which you've been t... The holiday you are planning ... big success, in spite of a slight d... (obscure) — double-check your boo... ings.

GEMINI (May 21 — June 20)
Your predeliction for the easy way could land you in trouble, especially if it's a "big deal" you've allowed yourself to be talked into by an acquaintance. Honesty will definitely be the best policy. Unattached Geminis have a very ... a serious

...fitable deal, is imminent.

LEO (July 23 — Aug. 22)
Your business interests have been progressing well up until now, but for the next week or two be especially cautious and consider carefully before making decisions. Prepare for your work-load to increase greatly after the ...iddle of the month. Home life will be

...3 — Sept. 22)
...s and frustrations ...erstandings, so ...d than ever to ...siveness. Pro-...l head, it will ...g and selling, ...the greater

... Nov. 22)
... too seriously ...n, with embar-...Haughtiness and ...ut someone who ...ckfire. Rather than ...us faults, why don't ...em? But expect a ...se near the end of the

SAGITTARIUS (Nov. 23 — Dec. 21)
Your work should go well for you this month, provided you maintain your usual diligence. Be careful how you criticize another's carefully conceived plans; they won't appreciate it and will make no bones about telling you so. First reports of bad news will turn out to have been exaggerated.

Here are some comments:

a My friend says I'm stupid, but I buy the newspaper with the most interesting horoscopes.

b Do you know – some people actually make a life study of this rubbish? And make a fortune! Disgusting ...

c For years I never bothered with my stars but recently the predictions seem to be coming true.

d Our Alice read her horoscope and just after that she won £1,900 on the pools. Can't deny that, can you?

e I'm a practical person. Don't have enough time for dreams and self-indulgence. Get on with work, that's what I say.

f Funny you should ask me that. I've just joined a Keep Fit class and my horoscope said I should.

g I've never really felt that I was a true Scorpio. I'm more like a Libra.

h As a scientist, I deal in facts. Predictions should be based on research.

i Can't say that I believe them, but they're good for a laugh.

Analysis and discussion

a What questions do you think were asked?

b How would you have answered those questions?

c Do you feel that the date, time and place of your birth have an influence on your life or determine your future?

d How seriously would you take advice given by an astrologist?

e Why do you think so many people are fascinated by this way of seeking counsel?

f If you were troubled, where would you seek counsel?

6 Shall I tell you about it?

Introduction

Language students are often asked to 'describe' their rooms or 'talk about' a recent holiday. These exercises are intended to encourage the student to produce and use 'appropriate' descriptive words.

However, descriptions and reporting both depend upon perception, memory and appropriate and common interpretations of the meanings of descriptive words and phrases. We only have to study the following proverbs to realise how much our interpretation is affected by our attitudes and values:

– Seeing is believing.
– Out of sight, out of mind.
– Absence makes the heart grow fonder.

In this unit, there will be opportunities to practise accurate reporting skills and to check and compare impressions with other students.

---

1 Listening activity 1

a Before listening to the tape, study the drawings and, on your own, find one adjective which describes each facial expression.
b Look at the photographs and discuss the probable occupations and ages of the subjects.
c Follow the taped instructions you are about to hear. Make sure that you have a sheet of lined paper and a pen or pencil.

A Analysis

a   What did you find difficult or ambiguous about the instructions?

b   How could the instructions have been made clearer?

c   What assumptions were made as to common interpretations?

B Discussion

Listen to the tape again to check and discuss your answers.

a   Compare your answers with those of other students.

b   How and why do they differ?

c   What conclusion can you draw as to the principles of giving clear instructions?

2   Reading activity 1

Jolly & Roger, South London estate agents, are advertising these properties. Match the descriptions with the photographs.

a
Ideal for the busy young executive. No garden or maintenance. Near Balham Station, BR and Tube. Private entrance and telephone.

b
For the first-time buyer. Desirable residential area. Close to shops and transport. In need of some improvement and decorating. Bargain!

c
Are you and your family running out of space? Aren't there times when you'd like some peace and quiet? If so, this is the house for you. Completely private without being isolated. There is a garage for the family car and plenty of room for the kids' bikes.

d
If you are approaching retirement, you'll be thinking about the quiet life. What could be better than a lovely country cottage? Nothing to disturb you but the sounds of birds. Roses growing round the front door. The vegetables you've planted providing tasty meals throughout the year. A well-earned haven!

A Analysis

a Compare your answers with those of other students.

b What words in the advertisements link up with the photographs?

c How honest are the verbal descriptions?

B Discussion

a Describe the area where you are living at the moment.

b Compare it with the place where you were brought up.

c Working in groups, make a list of all the descriptive words used by members of the group.

d Discuss what these words mean to other members of the group.

3 Writing activity

You have received a birthday gift voucher for £25. The conditions are that you must use your voucher within 30 days and order from the firm mentioned.

Study the order form and the descriptions of the articles. Decide what you would like to order and fill in the form. *Note:* all orders are subject to availability. If goods cannot be supplied, you will be credited with the amount and alternative goods can be ordered to the same value.

ORDER FORM

To: The Country Kitchen, Binns Close, Coventry CV4 9UJ. Tel: 0203 473934

PAYMENT
I enclose a cheque/PO payable to
The Country Kitchen for £ _____
OR
Please charge my Access/Visa card No.

Total amount of order £ _____
Cardholder's
Signature _____

Mr/Mrs/Miss _____
Address _____
_____
_____ Post Code _____

Phone
Number

	Item Code Number	Item Description (as in Catalogue)	Col/ Size	Qty	Item Price	Total Price £ p
e.g.	X 325	*Super Bowl*	—	1	3.95	3.95
	X				£	
	X				£	
	X				£	
	X				£	
	X				£	
	X				£	
	X				£	
	X				£	
	X				£	
	X				£	
	X				£	
	X				£	

Do you have a friend who would like to receive our catalogue FREE?

NAME _____

ADDRESS _____

_____
_____ POST CODE _____

TOTAL COST OF ORDER	
Postage & Packing: Add £1.95 (£2.95 orders over £25)	
Offshore surcharge to non-mainland destination extra £3	
Sub Total	
Less voucher if applicable	
TOTAL PAYABLE	

THE COPPER COOKWARE RANGE

Gleaming copper outside — stainless steel inside.
A very high quality range of continental cookware from Berry. It uses four materials **copper** outside for its attractive lustre and even heat distribution; **stainless steel** inside which is tough, hygienic and easy to clean; **aluminium** in the middle of the sandwich for lightweight thermal efficiency; and **brass** for the solid traditional riveted handles. Made to last for years — and offered at a very reasonable price.

Butter Pan 4¾"
£12.95   X313

Saucepans with Lid
£22.95	X309	5½"
£28.95	X310	6¼"
£39.95	X311	8"

Complete Set of Three Saucepans
£89.95   X312

Frying Pan 9½"
£22.95   X315

Casserole 8"
£39.95   X314

Storage Jars
The whole range has been made in fine ironstone pottery in Stoke-on-Trent. **Buy the whole set of 11 Jars at a special price,** or whatever combination suits your needs.

Very Large 8" Jars
Flour	X004	Biscuits	X006
Rice	X005	Cereal	X007
Each	**£7.95**		
Set of 4	**£29.95**		X008

Medium 5½" Jars
Tea	X009	Sugar	X011
Fruit	X010	Coffee	X012
Each	**£5.95**		
Set of 4	**£19.95**		X013

Small 4" Jars
Honey	X014	Jam	X016
Marmalade	X015		
Each	**£4.95**		
Set of 3	**£13.95**		X017

Complete Set of Storage Jars
£59.95   X018

Yoghurt Maker
£12.95   X115
The natural way to make your own yoghurt. The kit includes a **milk server** so you can simmer milk without it boiling over, a **special thermometer** showing only the marks you need for easy yoghurt making, an **insulated jar** which has exactly the right incubation characteristics and is good-looking enough to serve the final product in **plus** an instruction and recipe leaflet. A pair with the Soft Cheese Maker.

Professional Kitchen Knives

Superb kitchen knives from Kitchen Devil in Sheffield. Crafted in the finest stainless steel to retain a sharp cutting edge and resist corrosion. Beautifully balanced handles with brass rivets. A joy to work with.

Basic Set
8¼" Carver
£9.95   X059

5¾" Cooks Knife
£8.95   X060

3½" Vegetable Knife
£4.95   X061

Complete Set in Gift Box
£22.50   X062

6" Boning Knife
£9.95   X063

2½" Paring Knife
£4.75   X064

7" Filleting Knife
£9.95   X065

4 Reading activity 2

Michelle Joyce, aged 9, attends a primary school in Inner London. She has been on a day trip to Chartwell and has written the report opposite. Michelle has given permission for her report to be reproduced.

A Analysis

Imagine that you are Michelle's teacher.

a Correct the spelling.

b Evaluate her experience: What are her priorities? What was she impressed by? How much do you think she learned?

B Discussion

a How important do you think it is to spell accurately?

b What is the difference between a child's perceptions and those of an adult?

c Can you remember a similar experience as a child? What impression did the experience make on you?

This is a project for my teacher.
One day last week I went in a big coach to a
famous Place. And we went on a motorway.
The map says A2. After that we went to a
Place called sevenoaks but I dont no why.
I didn't see sevenoaks. After that we
went on a smaller road and it was very
wineding. Joe was sick but I wasate.
Then there was a sign. It said chartwell.
Good. We can have our Picknik. But we
didn't. We walked. It is a very big Place.
There are ducks and swans and sheep.

Allso fish. The fish are orange and black
and Joe was afraid of them. Joe is
nice but stipid. The Garden is enumous.
Very very big. My legs hert. Then
we had our picknik. And we quied
up for Ices. Joe wanted a choc Ice
but there was ownlee one So I had
orange. I dont like orange. Then we
went to the house. My teacher had
the tictets. He was nerves. Frank
and Henry are rough and could
break up this famous Place. I thort it
would be boring but it wasate. It was
small. Good. Also there were medalls
and you unforms. Caroline was stipid.
She looked at Pictures. Her Project
will be boring. My Project is Good.
Isn't it then we went to the coach.
Joe wasate sick. I had sayages
at home. The End.

5 Listening activity 2

Listen to the interview and complete the
following statements.

a Amalia Rodrigues works overtime because . . .
b Her reasons for starting a Saturday School
   were . . .
c Parents of bi-cultural children in Britain can
   feel . . .
d Bi-cultural children themselves may need . . .
e Amalia's ideas for the future of the Saturday
   School are . . .

6 Attitudes in Britain

Are you happy living where you do? Do you ever
dream about changing your lifestyle?

Look at the comments below on city life and
country life.

a Cor. I always thought milk came from bottles.

b Why is it you can never find a decent newspaper in the country?

c People are ever so friendly, aren't they? Never in a hurry.

d I'm fed up with school buses and waiting. Nothing ever happens here.

e Don't know how they can breathe with all that pollution.

f All right for a day trip, but that quiet would get on my nerves.

g Don't be ridiculous, Harriet. I couldn't commute from here.

h Look at that notice. Pick your own apples. Let's have a go, George.

Analysis and discussion

a Which of the speakers are city-dwellers?
   Which of them live in the country?
b How many of them do you think were just
   passing through?

c Where would (do) you choose to live – in a
   city or in the country? Describe the
   advantages and the drawbacks.
d Describe your ideal lifestyle. Compare and
   discuss your ideas with other people in the
   group.

7 How can I explain?

Introduction

To get out of awkward situations, you need sensitivity and sophisticated language skills. First, you have to identify the real problem. Then, you have to try to understand the feelings and points of view of others involved in the situation. Then you have to find the strategies and appropriate language needed to resolve the situation.

Often, all that is needed is a clear explanation. At other times, it may be necessary to apologise. Sometimes, an apology is not enough and an offer to repair the situation is needed too.

In this unit, you will have opportunities to identify problems, decide on strategies and practise appropriate language.

---

1 Listening activity 1

Look at each photograph and begin to imagine yourself in such a situation. How would you feel? How would you behave?
Listen to other people who are trying to get out of awkward and difficult situations.

First, identify the problem.
Then decide whether each speaker is:
a   giving a plausible reason
b   making an excuse
c   apologising
d   apologising and suggesting a remedy.

A Analysis

a   What words or phrases helped you to decide what the situation was?
b   How many of the speakers used formal language? Why did they do so?

B Discussion

a What would you say to a traffic warden who was writing out a ticket to put on your parked car?

b What would you say to a bank manager who had caused you inconvenience and embarrassment?

c How would you deal with a ticket collector who told you that you had no right to be travelling in a first-class compartment?

2 Reading activity 1

Look at the illustrations and discuss:

a the reasons for the apologies
b who the apologies are aimed at
c how members of the public might react.

Read this short letter. Analyse and discuss:

d how much the letter explains
e what the writer is apologising for
f what the reaction of the recipient might be.

Smith and Partners apologise for any inconvenience caused whilst this building is being renovated.

UNDER NEW MANAGEMENT
Please bear with us while we make improvements for the benefit of all our customers.

AKV construction apologise for any traffic delays while the road is being widened

This office is temporarily closed and will not re-open until Monday morning. We apologise for any inconvenience to our clients.

Monday 2nd

Dear Enid,
Sorry I haven't written before. Things haven't been good and, honestly, I couldn't decide what to say. The fact is that I won't be able to live up to my promises. If I'd had just that bit of luck... Don't give up. There's always another day. And I still love you. Don't write to me. I'll write to you.

Yours
Albert

3 Writing activity

It is important to recognise the appropriateness of apologies, reasons for making them and offers to make amends, but it is also necessary for the person receiving the apology to decide how to respond.
– Should the apology be accepted or rejected?
– How firm and assertive should the response be?
The answers to these questions depend on individual reactions to the situation.

Read this letter; decide how you would react if you received it; respond in writing. The words and phrases on the right might help you reply.

Acceptance
appreciated/interest
informed opinion
prompt response
personal note

Rejection
lack of personal touch
commercialism
no concern for customer/little follow-up
sense of responsibility

FREEWAYS Ltd.
The small car specialist

13 Aug. 1986

Dear Sir/Madam,

We regret any inconvenience caused by the recent breakdown of your car. Unfortunately the vehicle was no longer under full guarantee and we submit an estimate for parts and labour costs overleaf.

You may feel that as you have owned the car for 3 years, and as parts and labour will come to an amount approximating the value of the vehicle, it would be in your best interest to consider the purchase of another vehicle.

We must further inform you that our Service Department cannot undertake any major repair work for the next month due to the unusual demands on our services.

Should you wish to consider replacing your vehicle, please contact our specialist salesman, Bill Launder.

If, on the other hand, you have any queries about your present vehicle, do not hesitate to get in touch with me.

Yours faithfully

J W Till.

J W Till
(Managing Director)

---

4 Reading activity 2

Members of the public who are dissatisfied with the care they
receive under the National Health Service (NHS) in Britain can
complain through official channels. Each complaint will be
investigated. In some cases, findings will be published and
conclusions drawn based on the facts. This is a typical report:

Case No M222/33–34

Failure in care and communication

The complainant's mother was admitted to hospital after a fall. Her injuries were
considered to be superficial although there was considerable bruising. The
complainant expected her mother to be discharged from hospital within two
days and thus made appropriate arrangements for transport and home care.

  On visiting her mother the day following the accident, the complainant found
that her mother's condition had deteriorated. The mother, aged 82, seemed to be
confused and breathless. The complainant then asked to speak to someone in
charge. After waiting for 30 minutes, she repeated the request. Finally, as the
mother appeared to be resting, she decided to return to her home.

  Upon arriving home, she rang the hospital for reassurance about the condition
of her mother. The nurse on duty informed her that her mother was in theatre
for emergency surgery, as complications had developed. The duty nurse was
unable to give more information.

  The complainant states that she had left her telephone number and had asked
to be informed of any change in her mother's condition. This request had not
been complied with.

  On the day following the alleged surgical intervention, the complainant again
visited her mother. The mother's condition appeared unchanged and there was
no indication that she had undergone surgery.

  The complainant states that she was able to consult a senior nurse on duty,
who disclaimed all knowledge of any emergency surgery. There was no written
record of such action.

A Analysis
a Read the report and list the daughter's
   grounds for complaint.
b How would you describe the style of the
   report:
   – carefully written
   – officialese
   – meticulous attention to detail
   – objective
   – biased?
c What words or phrases can you find to
   support your description?

B Discussion
a If you were the complainant in similar
   circumstances, what channel of complaint
   would you choose:
   telephone   letter   personal encounter?
b As a member of the hospital staff, what
   reasons/excuses/apologies could you offer to
   repair the situation?

C Roleplay
Work in groups of three or four to represent the
parties concerned. One of the group should act
as an observer, make notes and report back.

🔁 5   Listening activity 2

Listen to the first part of this telephone conversation and decide:

a   what the subject of the conversation is
b   what the relationship of the speakers is.

Listen to the second part of the conversation and follow the caller's instructions.

🔁 6   Attitudes in Britain

The Chancellor of the Exchequer is required to explain and justify the Government's Budget to Parliament and to the public, represented by Members of Parliament. The 'mini-budget', usually announced in the autumn, is seldom noticed by the public. However, the major Budget speech proposes levels of personal taxation, corporation tax, inheritance tax, tax on unearned income . . . and so it goes on. The Chancellor must also address himself to specifying ways of raising revenue, such as through road tax on vehicles, duty on cigarettes and alcohol, VAT on a wide range of consumer goods and services.

There is a sort of fever among members of the British public prior to the Chancellor's major Budget speech. Here are some examples of what is said before 'The Budget'.

a   I'm sure he's going to up tax on fags. I've bought 40 cartons. Mind you, I had to queue up.

b   As a motorist and a representative of motorists, I refuse to believe that he would countenance a further increase in road tax.

c   Never mind wine. What I want is a real pint at a realistic price.

d   *We* don't like it. *They* don't like it. We know we're not competitive. But what can you do? A room in the West End has to make a profit. Gets worse every year . . .

e   It's always the same. The night before the Budget, the same surburbanites fill their tanks. How much can you save that way? Took me two hours to get home last night.

f   I recommend heavy taxes on sweets and chocolates. Tooth decay is a source of pain and expenditure.

g   With a bit of luck, the mortgage rates will go down. Even half a percent would help. We might take the kids on a holiday.

h   I'm sure they think that people like me don't matter. Not contributing, am I? But I *did* – for 40 years. Now that I'm out of sight, I just hope I shan't be forgotten.

Analysis and discussion

a   All of the speakers had a particular interest in the Budget. What do you think their particular concerns were?

b   Why were the speakers so interested in these particular aspects of the Budget? What changes in their lives might occur if their predictions became reality?

c   What are the necessities for a comfortable, happy life? How many of your 'necessities' are, or should be, taxed?

d   What do you consider to be necessities rather than luxuries? For example, is soap a necessity . . .   or toothpaste . . .   or disinfectant . . .   or bread and butter?

8 Do we understand each other?

Introduction

Without understanding, people have a strong tendency to jump to conclusions, make uninformed judgements and decisions, and arrive at a point of confrontation. This can be confirmed by parents and children, husbands and wives, employers and employees, politicians, and diplomats the world over. In fact, it can occur in almost every area of life.

In this final unit, a consolidation unit, you will be asked to use the skills that have been practised in earlier units. There will also be an opportunity to practise summarising and re-phrasing. You will be able to demonstrate how well you can interpret what you see, read and hear. You will be able to prove to yourself that you can cope with a variety of situations – in English.

1 Listening activity 1

The photographs present scenes of confrontation and aggression. What, in your opinion, might have caused these situations to develop? How might it have been possible to avoid confrontation?

Listen to four examples of potentially explosive situations. Can you suggest more constructive ways of dealing with the particular problems?

A Analysis

a In the dialogues you have just heard, how many of the speakers began with confrontation?
b What sort of questions were asked – aggressive and accusing; open and interested; information-seeking?

B Discussion

a How would you have behaved if you had been:
   Claudia, Charlie, Miss Phillips, Tom?
b What answers would you have given to the questions asked?
c How could the questions have been phrased to avoid confrontation?
   For example:
   What have you done with my car keys?

   A more appropriate question might be:
   I've mislaid my keys again, Claudia. Have you seen them?

2   Reading activity 1

Here are two notices taken from different noticeboards. Read the notices carefully, paying attention to the language used.

A Analysis

How are the verbs,
must–can–may–could–should used –
a to invite   c to order
b to suggest   d to negotiate?
e Who were the notices directed towards?

B Discussion

Compare your findings with those of some fellow students.

C Roleplay

Work in pairs. One person should take the role of the 'accuser' and the other the role of the 'accused'. Ask the sort of questions you heard on the tape. Discuss your reactions.

Now change roles. The role of the questioner now is to understand the problem and give the other person an opportunity to respond helpfully and positively.

How well did you manage to solve the problem? Was a co-operative, rather than an aggressive approach more helpful?

It has come to the attention of the Headmaster that school premises have been used for unscheduled activities. These premises are the property of the Education Board and all meetings must be cleared through and approved by the Headmaster's Office. Under no circumstances can any meeting take place without prior arrangement and approval.

Michael Billington
Headmaster

COME ONE... COME ALL...

It's your get-together. COHSE says you can come and you may bring a friend. You could join us soon. In fact, you'll feel you should.

Now read this memo, addressed to senior managers. The words underlined could be interpreted in more than one way.

MEMO

FROM   The Managing Director

TO   All Senior Managers

SUBJECT Submission of items for inclusion on the agenda, Managing Director's meeting, Friday 13 January.

All Senior Managers are expected to attend the Managing Director's meeting on Friday 13 January. Points on the agenda will include return on shares anticipated in the coming year.

Those Managers who wish to express extreme opinions should submit items for the agenda by Friday 6 January. Although all points of view will be considered, decisions must not be delayed.

Analysis and discussion

a Working on your own, try to determine the meaning of the words underlined in the context of the memo.

b Replace the words underlined with other words or phrases. Change other parts of the memo as necessary, but do not change the meaning.

c In groups, compare different versions of the memo. Discuss the reason(s) for any differences.

d What English words and phrases have caused *you* confusion?

3   Writing activity

Write a report, in the form of a letter, evaluating an aspect of your job or studies.

a Express any:
  – anxieties
  – criticisms
  – satisfactions
  – dissatisfactions
  – suggestions for improvement.

b Decide:
  – who to write to
  – what to say
  – how to say it.

c Try to:
  – remember the point of view of the person you are writing to
  – separate information(facts) and opinions clearly
  – use a format acceptable to the recipient.

d Try to avoid:
  – asking unanswerable questions
  – being aggressive rather than assertive
  – expressing yourself ambiguously.

4 Reading activity 2

Diaries, or journals, are a source of information and interest for
historians, sociologists, geneaologists and the reading public. These
accounts, while containing the impressions of the writer, provide a
record of facts and events which might otherwise have been lost.
Even in the early 20th century, children were encouraged to keep
diaries and were given leather-bound books for Christmas. There
was, of course, a lock and key, so that any secrets could remain
secret. Unfortunately, secrets are almost invariably revealed!

Read the following excerpts from the diary of a 14-year-old girl.
The entries were made between 1930 and 1931.

Sunday
A miserable day. M and F. silent. F. very
late last night, apparently. M. and I went to
church. Saw Phyllis wearing complete new
outfit. Didn't see Henry. Oh dear, has he
forgotten me? M. says that there are other
fish in the sea. What have fish to do with
me and my love? Sunday dinner was a
disaster. F. told M. that the soup was
cold and the joint was tough and the
table was without condiments. M. said
that if F. wasn't happy, he could go back
to his mistress ???? F. got very angry then
and accused M. of turning his only child
against him. The only child must be me. I
am determined to discover what a mistress
is and how you turn a child.

Tuesday
School, of course. Miss T. very pleased
with my poem. Miss W. rude about map
of S. Africa. Miss W. is always rude about
my maps. She likes Phyllis. I don't.
Saw Phyllis talking to Henry. Horrid
girl. M. very loving but quiet. F. away
again.

Friday
End of term. Hurrah! No more Phyllis.
Christmas in 10 days. Have decided
not to become a famous actress. It is as
M. says, a cheap and tawdry profession.
Tawdry???? How could I be a real
Ophelia when that silly Phyllis was
Hamlet? F. home but very quiet. M.
quiet too. What hopes for a merry
Christmas?

Dear Diary, I shan't be writing
again. F. told M. that our life was
over. There is a depression ???? and
F. has sold our house to pay the
debts. He says we are lucky to be able
to eat. He says many people can't.
M. says he has been a spendthrift
and unfaithful. F. says that M. was
the spendthrift and why does she go
on running up accounts. M. says
that she needs something to make
her happy when her husband prefers
other feminine company. F. says
that any company is better than
hers. M. sobs. F. slams the door.
What shall I do?

Dear Diary, This is the last and
final message. M and I are moving
to a flat. F. is going to S. Africa to
seek his fortune. I cried when he
kissed me. Stupid for a grown-up
young lady. I am stupid. So I'm
going to a new school. M. says that
the children are not suitable for
friends. How does she know? And
why does she call them 'children'?
Au revoir, dear diary.

A Analysis and discussion

a List the expressions which the diarist does not seem to understand.
  How would you explain them to Jennifer, the diarist?

b Who do you think these people were:
  – M   – Henry
  – F   – Miss T
  – Phyllis   – Miss W?

c When did Jennifer first appear to notice signs of family unrest?

d What effect did these first indications have on her?

e What evidence is there to suggest that Jennifer attended a girls' school?

f What can you find in the diary which might suggest one explanation for the problems in Jennifer's family?

B Roleplay and discussion

a Work in small groups. One student should take the role of F and another, M. Both may refer to the diary. Other members of the group should act as observers. Suggest ways in which confrontation and conflict might have been eased or avoided.

b Two observers then take the roles of F and M. Try to give this story a happier ending.

5 Listening activity 2

Listen to this recording which was made in the boardroom of a multi-national company. The matters discussed include questions of redundancy, early retirement, investment and pensions.

A Analysis

a How many members of the board attended the meeting?
b How much money did the late start cost the company, according to the Chairman?
c Why was the late start so expensive?
d Who had to pay for it?
e What was Miss Guest's job?
f What position did Joe Tait hold?
g How did Helen Heatherington manage to take control of the meeting?

B Discussion

a How did you feel about the Chairman's attitude towards his 'team' and workforce?
b What is your assessment of the attitude of the 'team' to the Chairman?
c Why did the Board reach a point of confrontation?
d Who was in control at the end of the meeting?
e What do you think will happen at the next meeting?

6 Attitudes in Britain

The word 'work' has a variety of meanings and interpretations. In some societies, where work is seen as an end in itself, those who do not work are unacceptable. In other societies, work is seen as a means of producing money for leisure and survival.

Public attitudes to work influence social and government policies on a wide range of issues: unemployment benefits, employment priorities, education, the provision of leisure facilities, day nurseries for the children of working parents . . .
  Read this cross-section of comments collected during a survey of attitudes to work in Britain.

a Why would they want to work when they can get more for sitting about? I've been commuting for 20 years ... since my 17th birthday. I've earned every penny I have. I've worked weekends and evenings and I've never asked for overtime ...

b If the Government was happy to support me, I wouldn't go to work either. Only two years to go to the pension and, believe me, I'm taking life easy.

c I'm redundant at 56. I tried to hide it for a long time ... from the family and the neighbours. I knew they would think I'd disgraced them. When I applied for jobs, they said, 'Sorry, you're over-qualified'. What they meant was, 'You're too old'.

d I'm happy to give you my opinion. And here's an example. In all my 40 years, I've never seen anything so disgraceful as that young man next door. His poor little wife goes out to work six days a week. I see her catching the 7.10 bus. And what is he doing? Feeding the kids and getting them off to school. A man doing a woman's work.

e I speak from my experience of 30 years in Parliament. Full employment is a thing of the past. In the near future, we shall have to adjust to, and provide for, job-sharing, early retirement and leisure activities.

f You've come to the right place, haven't you mate? I've been a regular at this Job Centre since I left school 18 months ago. If they ever call my name, I don't think I'd recognise it.

g Have you had a look at all those jobs in the evening paper? I ask you – all those jobs advertised and they say we have 62,000 unemployed in this area. They want to set their alarms, make themselves smart and get up and go. That's what I did 20 years ago and I was only 15.

h My father's an engineer – with a degree. Now he spends his time growing beans on a smallholding. The beans are good – but boring. And he's bored, I can tell ... What's the use of school when nobody cares how much you know? What's the point of A-levels? I could leave at 16 and get a job to help out.

A Analysis

a How many of the speakers were probably unemployed?

b How many of the speakers were:
 – under 30
 – between 50 and 60
 – over 60?

c What questions were asked in the survey?

B Discussion

a What sort of work do you consider to be:
 – vital   – desirable
 – important   – unnecessary?

b Are wages related to job importance?

c What sort of work would you consider to be 'women's' work? What sort of work is 'men's' work? Give examples.

d How important is your work to you?
 – Is it the centre of your life?
 – Do you see it as a career?
 – How easy would it be to change jobs?

e If your working hours were reduced by 50 per cent, how would you use your leisure time?

f If you lost your job, what would be the attitude of:
 – your family   – your friends?

Tapescript and Notes

Unit One

Listening activity 1

IMMIGRATION OFFICER: Where do you come from?
  Where have you come from?
  How long do you plan to stay?
  Have you got a return ticket?
  Are you seeking employment?
LANDLADY: You must be hungry. Tell me what you'd
  like for breakfast.
  How much do you know about Shenfield?
  What made you decide to come here?
  While you're here, what would you like to see and
  do?
  It must have been a very long flight. How did you
  amuse yourself?

Listening activity 2

ANNOUNCER: Here is Patrick Simmons with another
  edition of Medicine for You. Our subjects tonight:
  Should smoking be left to the smoker? Why patients
  are not told about the side effects of prescribed
  medicines. The dangers of jogging.
PATRICK SIMMONS: Now – should smokers have the right
  to choose whether to smoke at all; if so, where and
  when? How dangerous is smoking, not only for the
  smoker, but for the non-smoker who has no choice

but to inhale others' fumes? It might be sensible for
you, the listener, smoker or non-smoker, to have a
close look at the advantages and disadvantages and
weigh them up.
I look forward to receiving your comments on the
questions raised.
Now to the questions:
Perhaps you find smoking adds to your pleasure –
cigarette or cigar with your after-dinner coffee, for
example.
Does smoking calm you down?
Does smoking keep you from eating between
meals?
Does smoking give you social confidence?
Does smoke cling to your breath and clothing?
Do you find that, as a smoker, you are the odd one
out?
What about exercise: jogging, or swimming, or
climbing stairs – do you fight for breath?
I've neglected to mention money: how much could
you save if your money weren't going up in smoke?
I need hardly mention what is, perhaps, the most
important argument – the health risk: lung cancer,
emphysema, heart disease, circulatory disorders.
The list is alarmingly long.
So, to smoke or not to smoke. The decision is yours.
And now, a change of subject . . .

Notes

Introduction

Use the Introduction – in every Unit – to set the scene.
Give and get the students to give examples of friendly
questions (e.g. 'While you're here, what would you like
to see?'), official questions (e.g. 'What is your name'),
etc. Discuss contrasting intonation with the same
question, e.g.: Can I help you? spoken by a friend/
shop assistant/salesperson/doctor/policeman, etc. Get
the students to give different forms of the same
question, e.g. friendly/formal/official.

Listening activity 1

Students should be encouraged to listen to each
person as necessary before answering A Analysis.
Students should work in pairs and compare answers
and reasons before discussing their interpretation with
the whole class. Let the class listen to the speakers
again before answering.

B Discussion Note that the Discussion allows the
class to recognise some of the attitudes noted in the
Introduction – friendly, official, etc.

Reading activity 1

Give an example of an implied question, e.g. Income:
Do you earn enough to join the scheme? Students can
work in pairs or small groups on A Analysis. Discuss
answers with the class allowing for different
possibilities. The class can do B Discussion in small
groups before having an exchange of views with the
whole class.

Writing activity

When students fill in Section A of the form, emphasise
accuracy and legibility. Section B of the form: ask the
class what the nurse's attitude might be – gentle/
reassuring/distant, etc? Students can work in pairs on
this part of the form, discussing possible questions
before reporting back to the whole class for
comparison and discussion of the questions.

B Discussion can be a class discussion. Students
should be encouraged to think of cultural differences/
taboo questions/situational differences, etc.

C Roleplay Get the class to discuss the questions and responses given, noting the distinction between the first three (Direct) and the last three (Indirect). Get the students to work in pairs to prepare five further questions and responses, both direct and indirect. Ask the class to comment on several pairs' questions and responses with respect to appropriacy/situation/level of formality, etc.

Listening activity 2

Discuss headline language with the class, e.g. length, choice of phrase/word, size of print, etc. Get the class to read the article and say what they think about the style (e.g. Is the reporting factual? Is comment or opinion included?) and the choice of language (e.g. Is it formal or colloquial? What sort of newspaper would it appear in – the quality or popular press?) Ask the students to suggest a suitable headline and give reasons for their choice.

Get the students to do A Analysis in pairs.

Key
a A lot ('endless')
b six altogether ('Is the House aware . . . ?' etc)
c hunt, wipe out, attacks, predatory, exterminated, slaughtered, butchery, destroyed.
d show – display; completely – systematically; type – species; destroyed – exterminated; cruel – merciless; obviously – openly.

B Discussion can be done in pairs or groups, then with the whole class. Students should be encouraged to compare the style of this article with journalistic styles in their countries.

Reading activity 2

Check that the students know how to take notes – information words, abbreviations, symbols, etc. Let the class listen to the tape at least twice while making notes for A Analysis. Check the points raised with the class. Get the students to write a simple summary containing the main points of the talk based on their notes and the list.

B Discussion   Divide the class into small groups containing only smokers or non-smokers. Get the groups to answer a, b and c, then have an open class discussion.

Attitudes in Britain

Impress on the students that this section presents a cross-section of opinions in Britain and does not attempt to present facts or statistics. Explain local/cultural references: Morden to Moorgate = a long way/City types . . . Barbican = the well-off. It may be useful, and fun, for the students to listen to the tape first before looking at the section in the book. Then let the students study the cartoon. The class can then listen to the cassette again while reading the statements, noting against each what sort of person might be speaking and whether they express approval or disapproval. Discuss the answers with the class.

Get the class to do the Analysis and Discussion, using dictionaries if they wish. Get the students to add to the list of adjectives where possible.

Unit Two

Listening activity 1*

MAN: Good morning, Are you in charge of the kitchen? If so, I think you should be aware that I have special requirements. I have no objection to dairy products or an occasional egg, but meat and fish are out of the question. I trust that you will be able to cope.

*MRS CRAWFORD: There is no question of preparing special diets for conference members unless they have given us advance notice. You'll have to take pot luck, I'm afraid, and leave anything you don't want. There will always be soup and salad. And bread, of course.

MISS STONE: Hello. You must be Mrs Crawford. My name's Cynthia Stone and I sent you a special diet form. Hope it arrived on time. Anyway, I can't eat meat or fish but I love vegetables and salad. And I'm looking forward to tasting your famous risotto.

*MRS CRAWFORD: Welcome to the seminar, Miss Stone.

It was very helpful of you to tell us your special requirements. We have some lovely vegetarian dishes planned for you – including some risotto, of course.

*These two sections are recorded once only. The first part of the recording includes only the Man's and Miss Stone's statements, the second part as scripted above.

Listening activity 2

WOMAN: It's not good enough. It's just not good enough! You've let me down again.

MAN: Relax, will you?

WOMAN: Relax! You're the expert on relaxation. Give me some lessons, why don't you? Of course, you'll need to have a rest first.

MAN: Oh, come one, Helen. Calm down. It's not my fault if you've had a hard day at the office. Why don't you have a cup of tea?

WOMAN: *In* what?

MAN: In a mug, of course.

WOMAN: All the mugs and cups are piled up in the sink. Dirty. And there's no milk.

MAN: So? It's not the end of the world. I think there's half a lemon and I can rinse out a mug. You can have some lemon tea.

WOMAN: Don't bother. The effort might exhaust you.

MAN: This isn't getting us anywhere. What is the problem?

WOMAN: Right. Are you going to listen? Really listen? When we moved into this flat, we made a working arrangement. I was to carry on with my job. You were to keep the flat running and finish your book. We were going to be partners. Right?

MAN: Right.

WOMAN: Well, I think I've completed my part of the bargain.

MAN: Are you suggesting that I haven't?

WOMAN: Why don't you answer your own question?

MAN: Because it's too difficult. I admit that the place is a mess. We both know I haven't written a word for weeks. I just haven't been able to.

WOMAN: I can see you're unhappy and I'm not very happy either. At least we've said it. Do you agree that our 'working arrangement' isn't working?

MAN: Yes. I mean, no it isn't. *You're* working, but the arrangement isn't.

WOMAN: Oh, well. All arrangements can be changed. They're not binding. We can always have a rearrangement, can't we? And I *would* like some lemon tea.

Notes

Introduction

Ask the students if they have heard of assertiveness training (popular in Britain, especially as part of the Women's Movement). Establish the differences perceived in Britain between 'assertive' and 'aggressive'. Compare with attitudes in the students' own countries.

Listening activity 1

Use the menus to introduce and check vocabulary. Ask if food is an emotive subject in their countries. e.g. Is vegetarianism an issue? Get the class to read A Analysis. Play the cassette at least twice.

Note: Play the statements only. Get the students to discuss their answers in pairs.

Get the class to read B Discussion, using dictionaries to check the word list if they wish, before listening to the cassette.

Reading activity 1

Discuss with the class what advertisements do – inform/promote/recruit, etc, before doing the activity.

Key

Employer: Reuters; *Type of job:* Projects Executive; *Location:* Central London with travel to Europe and elsewhere; *Salary:* £12,000–£13,000; *Requirements:* Candidates must be numerate, capable of driving many simultaneous projects smoothly and achieving deadlines, a degree; *Advantages:* knowledge of financial markets, project management experience; *Career prospects:* excellent within Reuters; *Action to take* (if any): Telephone Mrs Boncal on 01-251 7095 or write to her at Reuters, 85 Fleet St, London EC4P 4AJ.

a	true	**d**	not true
b	true	**e**	not true
c	not true		

B Discussion Discuss the vocabulary, referring to the advertisement where possible. Get the students to discuss their answers in pairs before conducting a class survey and discussion.

C Roleplay: Let pairs decide which advertisement to work on. Get the 'Personnel Officers' to make notes on the qualities expected of an applicant and to think of questions (direct or indirect) to elicit that information (e.g. capable of directing/working on simultaneous projects/'How many courses were you able to take comfortably at University in each term?'). Get the applicants to make notes on their qualifications and experience, which should not be perfect in all areas.

Writing activity

Make sure that the students understand the layout and style of an English business letter: addresses, reference, date, salutation, conclusion, direct but polite style. If students choose **b,** their style should be less formal, e.g. no reference, less formal salutation and conclusion, less direct style, etc.

Reading activity 2

Do not reveal the origin of the passage (the American Declaration of Independence) until the end of the activity. Some examples of assertive expression: We hold these truths . . . with manly firmness . . . we have reminded them . . . .

Listening activity 2

Point out to the class that a different intonation can give a different meaning to a spoken utterance. Refer back to the Introduction to Unit 1 for examples. Also give the example **a** with different intonations. Play the cassette as many times as the class wish to enable them to discuss and answer the questions.

B Discussion Note that some students may find this an unusual situation and may have no direct experience of it. It may be useful to do the first part in small groups.

Attitudes in Britain

Before reading the responses, let the class listen to the cassette and say which responses indicated approval, which indicated disapproval, and which were difficult to understand, e.g. **e** may prove difficult because of the expression 'gang of lefties' (people with left-wing political ideas).

Unit Three

Listening activity 1
Telephone conversation 1
WOMAN: Yes, it was a bit of a shock, but we'll manage.
MAN: It won't be easy, will it? With Tom away. Can't I give Tony and Emma a lift to school when I drop our lot off?
WOMAN: Bless you. That *would* help. It should only be for a few days. The mechanic's just waiting for parts.
MAN: I've heard that before! Now, how are you getting to work?
WOMAN: Don't worry about me. I'll walk down to the station and hop on the train. Time I did some walking! Been carbound for months.
Telephone conversation 2
MAN: Could you just clarify that last point? Are you saying that those parts you promised me won't be arriving on Friday?
WOMAN: I suppose you could say that. There seems to be some trouble at the docks.
MAN: There's always trouble somewhere. Usually with *your* outfit. And, I can never get a categorical *yes* or *no*. All this beating about the bush . . . I don't know.
WOMAN: We're doing the best we can.
MAN: Your best isn't good enough. Do you realise that it's costing me a fortune in wages and goodwill? Mechanics hanging around doing nothing. Customers ringing up. It's no joke, you know.
WOMAN: Could you hang on a moment? I've just had a message saying that our consignment is on its way. Things should be easier . . .

Listening activity 2
ALEX: To conclude this week's *Good Books Programme,* we have asked Penny Double to give us her choice of recent publications. Penny, I believe you've chosen a novel without horror, crime or sensation . . . as you say. Can such a novel be a best-seller these days?
PENNY DOUBLE: I am not predicting sales, Alex. I was asked to talk about a good book I had recently read, and that's what I'm going to do. *Mrs Addlestone at Home* is the title and I found I could identify with the real human characters. Just listen to this passage describing Mrs Addlestone:
'Mrs Addlestone was a comfortable, middle-aged woman. She had worked hard all her life and that accomplishment gave her a great deal of satisfaction. She had managed to bring up a large family almost single-handed. She had just enough money to get by. And that was the greatest comfort of all.
In appearance, Mrs Addlestone was not at all remarkable. The sort of person you could pass without noticing. She was quite short, with nondescript hair. She was what is sometimes called "pleasantly plump".
However, in spite of this comfortable exterior, Alice Addlestone had certain worries. She was a heavy smoker . . . and was aware of the consequences. Her sons called her a typical woman driver and insisted that she use the car only for local driving. Her favourite daughter disapproved of her getting up so late. Now, Mrs Addlestone knew that her children meant well, but it was a worry . . .

Notes

Introduction

Discuss the different types of listening with the class with examples – a station announcement (facts and figures), a political discussion (interpreting attitudes), a TV report (overall understanding), etc.

Listening activity 1

Play each conversation several times before discussing answers with the class.

Key
Conversation 1
a   a car under repair

b getting children to school and mother to work
c friendly
d First names, offers of help, sympathy

Conversation 2
a waiting for spare parts
b no definite date, money and goodwill lost, mechanics with nothing to do, customers impatient
c unfriendly
d e.g.: 'trouble . . . usually with your outfit', 'Your best isn't good enough', etc.

Reading activity 1

Discuss the vocabulary with the class if necessary. After doing the activity, give and get the class to give further examples of situations where short messages can communicate efficiently, e.g. telephone messages, assembly instructions, etc.

Writing activity

Key
a 1 confirm; 2 discussions; 3 assembly; 4 delegates
b 1 overjoyed; 2 flat; 3 just right; 4 see.

Discuss contexts where the other words might be used to illustrate the formal/informal distinction. The distinction between the generalising word and the specifying word (residence/flat) should also be made.

Reading activity 2

Before the class reads *Passage 1,* discuss with them what they would do to ensure a child's safety in a car. *Passage 2* It will be obvious that the educational standard of the writer is not high — discuss with the class whether this could affect the quality of medical care received.

Listening activity 2

Discuss the introduction with the class. Ask the students what a normal working day is in their countries. Ask individual students what they feel is a long working day.
　　Possible ambiguous phrases from the talk: middle-aged; a large family; quite short; plump; a heavy smoker; her sons thought it was bad; late.

Attitudes in Britain

Students who have visited or are in Britain can add to the comments. Students should also be encouraged to discuss tourist expectations of their own countries and how this compares with the reality.

Unit Four

Listening activity 1

1
Oh, it's all so difficult. So much to think about, isn't there dear? I wonder whether I should go after all. I don't really *know* the grandchildren, do I? It's very good of them to ask me but . . . what about the heating . . . and the plants . . . and the cats? Suppose the milkman doesn't get my note? What if newspapers are left all over the doorstep? I'm sorry, Enid. Taking up so much of your time. I really must pull myself together. Now, where were we? Oh, yes. What needs to be done. I have a list somewhere. Here we are. Water and electricity. I'll turn them off. Oh, no. On second thoughts, you wouldn't be able to look after the plants. So leave water on. Do keep an eye on my African violets. They'll want watering from the bottom. Not too much water, mind you. Just keep them moist. What a good neighbour you are. If only my Alice was like you . . . I'll turn off the gas. Very dangerous to leave gas on you know. And will you pay attention to the weatherman? It would be dreadful if the pipes froze. Cleo and Henry are very independent when I'm here but I don't know how they will like an empty house. They don't drink milk, you know. Only sip soup. And they're very fond of sardines. There you are, Cleo. Naughty girl. Where have you been today? And where's your friend Henry? Oh, Enid. The children are waiting for you. Give them a kiss from Auntie. You are a real friend. Before you go, dear. Here's the key. You *will* look after it, won't you?

2
Whether you are well-travelled or going abroad for the first time, it's often useful to have someone to turn to for advice or guidance. We recommend that you check in for all flights at least 90 minutes before departure time. We must emphasise that failure to check in at recommended time may mean that you arrive after the airline has closed its check-in desk. If you miss your flight, it is your responsibility, but we will help you to get to your destination if we possibly can. Any arrangements that are made on your behalf will be at your expense and you will not be eligible for a refund on your original ticket.
　　On scheduled services of certain airlines, the hostesses do not usually offer duty free goods, so it may be wise to purchase those in advance at the airport.
　　Baggage allowances should be strictly adhered to.

Otherwise heavy surcharges will apply.

Please ensure that your Representative checks your return tickets soon after arrival so that there will be no difficulties with your flight home. Our specially trained Representatives or Agents are at all main resorts. Should there be any aspect of your holiday you are not completely satisfied with, please bring it to their attention.

Listening activity 2

Good evening, ladies and gentlemen. This is Antony Adams speaking to you from the Royal Festival Hall, on London's South Bank. Tonight's concert is rather special in that it combines the old and the new, with a performance of Sir Edward Elgar's Violoncello Concerto in E Minor, followed by the first broadcast of Henry Holmes' Electronic Expressions.

Elgar will be familiar to you all. His Cello Concerto was his final masterpiece. The first performance, given at Queen's Hall on October 26, 1919, with the composer conducting, was less than ideal and poorly supported. Fortunately for the audience tonight, the Cello Concerto soon recovered from the misfortunes of its first hearing and was recognised to be one of the greatest of all works for the cello.

Henry Holmes, the composer of Electronic Expressions, was born in Manchester, in 1964. His family was not at all musical. Indeed, he was discouraged from squeaking on the violin and blustering on the clarinet. Holmes was apprenticed to a large electrical company at the age of 16 and spent three years listening to the sounds and noises of industry . . . finding a stimulating rhythm and intriguing pitch. He now feels that he was fortunate in not having had a conventional musical training. His freedom of style has not been inhibited. Holmes went to to create his own instruments, free of the constraints that formal teaching might have engendered.

The London Paxharmonica Orchestra, together with their conductor, Ian McManus, have displayed great flexibility and tolerance in welcoming such an unusual work. And now . . . the audience is awaiting the arrival of Ian McManus.

Notes

Introduction

Give and get the students to give examples of messages which have gone astray, e.g. by playing 'Chinese Whispers' – start off a whispered message at one end of the class and see what changes have happened by the time it reaches the other end.

Key to the symbols CND, Roundabout, Children crossing, Stars for freezer, Traffic merges from the left, One-way street, Keep left, Do not iron, Pure new wool.

Listening activity 1

The first speaker is difficult to follow because she is nervous and is thinking as she goes along. The second has organised the information and is an experienced speaker.

Reading activity 1

Encourage the students to skim the brochure first with a time limit (e.g. 30 seconds) before reading it in detail, using their dictionaries if necessary.

C Roleplay It may be instructive as well as amusing to assign the tasks to students who are not confident of doing them. Give the students a few minutes to let them make notes on the chosen task. Subsequent discussion can provide further feedback for B Discussion.

Writing activity

Encourage the students to write in a fairly formal style such as might be found in a tourist brochure. Get the students to write brief notes first followed by clear comprehensive instructions.

Reading activity 2

Get the students to discuss the cartoons in small groups.

Key The early bird catches the worm – someone who acts promptly gets what he is after; there's no smoke without fire – all rumours have some foundation; a watched pot never boils – watching or being anxious about something won't hurry it up; too many cooks spoil the broth – too many people trying to help makes it impossible to get things done.

Explain the meanings of the proverbs and ask the students if they have similar ones in their own languages.

Ask the class to read the first sentence of the passage and establish what sort of story it will be. Discuss register/archaic language (e.g. 'great good fortune').

Key (A Analysis)
a paragraphs 1 and 2: archaic/formulaic language – were blessed with/perfect in every way/surpassed only by, etc; the situation; relatively simple syntax, etc.

b paragraph 3 – local family (King and Queen), village favourite (Princess); paragraph 5 – shopkeepers expected her to give them money . . . jobs and paragraph 6 (all).

Listening activity 2

Key

a combines the old and new
b Sir Edward Elgar
c electronic
d was not musical
e he did not have a conventional music training
f the new work is very unusual

Attitudes in Britain

If in Britain, take some examples of TV programmes for the day (from a newspaper) to class and get the students to study and discuss in pairs what type of programme is transmitted in the afternoon/at midday/ in the early evening/late at night. Compare the results with TV in the students' own countries. Explain that ITV is organised regionally and that BBC also has a few regional programmes. In Wales, some programmes are broadcast in Welsh. There is also cable TV in certain areas.

Unit Five

Listening activity 1

1

CUSTOMER: 'Dear Mr Crewe, we apologise for the late delivery of a part of your order.' Not again. Can't they even get my name right. 'Late delivery . . . part of order.' Don't understand what they're on about. 'Enquiries 006 5483.' Let's see how they deal with *my* enquiry. Hello, hello. My name's Crow.

VOICE: This is Consumicor Answering Service. When ordering one of our products, please give the catalogue number and description of the article. Orders can be placed between nine hundred hours and sixteen hundred hours. Quote your credit card number and . . .

CUSTOMER: Service. They call it service. Tomorrow I'll . . .

2

DAUGHTER: Is that Mercy Hospital? I'm ringing about my mother.

VOICE: Mercy Hospital.

DAUGHTER: Yes, I know. Have you got a Mrs Ethel Greene?

VOICE: What ward is she in?

DAUGHTER: Don't know, do I? That's why I'm ringing.

VOICE: When was the lady admitted?

DAUGHTER: Some time this afternoon. That's what the policeman said.

VOICE: Hmm. Emergency, I suppose. Have you tried A & E?

DAUGHTER: What's A & E? Is my mother there or isn't she? Why don't you answer my questions?

VOICE: I'm putting you through to A & E, caller.

3

TRAVELLER: Is that Liverpool Street Station? Can you tell me what time the last train leaves for Cambridge?

VOICE: One moment. I'll put you through to Enquiries.

2ND VOICE: Enquiries.

TRAVELLER: Can you tell me, please, what time the last train leaves for Cambridge?

2ND VOICE: Depends what day you're travelling. Weekends are different from weekdays. When are you going to Cambridge?

TRAVELLER: I'd been hoping to go today. That's why I'm ringing. It's urgent and . . .

2ND VOICE: Urgent, is it? Well, well, I'll have a look. The 23.14 gets in at 0.34. The 23.30 gets in at 0.48.

TRAVELLER: Will there be taxis if I arrive after midnight?

2ND VOICE: Nothing to do with us. You'll have to sort that out when you get there.

Listening activity 2

ANNOUNCER: Here is a special broadcast on behalf of the Society for the Protection of the Elderly. Speaking to you is Mary Gerard, a community nurse, herself 64 and suffering from arthritis.

MARY GERARD: Good evening and thank you for listening. Many people seem to believe that Britain's elderly and infirm are looked after in long-stay hospitals. In fact, 95 per cent of people over 65 live in the community, whether in their own homes or with their families. I thought it would be timely, as winter approaches, to ask you all to think about our rapidly increasing elderly population and focus on some of their needs and problems.

First, food. It is easy, especially if you're on your own, to neglect meals. One good meal a day is a must, with milk, fresh fruit and vegetables. Of course, all of us need some fish, meat, eggs or cheese. And please don't assume that everyone over 60 is incapable of shopping or cooking.

Encourage your elderly relatives or neighbours to do their own shopping as far as possible. Going down to the shops is good exercise, and we all enjoy a chat with our neighbours. One way of keeping in touch with local gossip, isn't it? The chemist's seems to be a gathering place. Not surprising. 'Swallow a tablet and you'll feel better.' That seems to be the attitude. But believe me, there's no truth in it.

Mrs Collins, one of the ladies I visit . . . well, that isn't her real name, but the story's true, . . . she's landed in hospital. What happened? Well, one day, she collected her prescription and walked home. It was a chilly day and she was a bit weary so she closed all the windows and lit the gas fire. Then she took a tablet and sat down to rest. She certainly rested but it's a good job I went in when I did. Gave the neighbours a shock when the ambulance arrived. Now, perhaps, they'll remember to drop in

from time to time and keep an eye on her . . . if she comes home, that is. They're good neighbours but they do forget. You know how it is. The other thing is that when I went in . . . she gave me a key . . . I couldn't see a thing. Can't afford to waste electricity. But I tripped on a rug and just managed to catch myself before I fell. Don't know how many times I've told her about that rug but her son Percy gave it to her.

ANNOUNCER: I am sorry to interrupt, Mary, but our time is up. Thank you Mary Gerard for reminding us of the particular problems of the elderly. And for sharing your experiences with us . . .

Notes

Introduction

Discuss with the class occasions when they have had difficulty in their own languages, particularly when under stress. Ask if they have experienced any problems when talking to someone from a different culture or in a foreign language.

Listening activity 1

Use the photographs for a discussion of cultural background as well as observation. *Note:* Post Offices in the UK are centres for many services – collecting pensions and family allowances, paying road tax, paying for TV licences and saving money. Postage stamps can normally be purchased only at Post Offices.

Play through all three telephone conversations before the students look at A Analysis. Then play each conversation separately, getting the students to make notes.

Key
a *Conversation 1:* calling to complain, gets only an answering service
Conversation 2: calling to enquire, gets confronted by terminology which is difficult to understand
Conversation 3: calling for information, gets slow unhelpful replies.
b unhelpful, confusing for the caller, indifferent attitudes, etc.
c probably unsatisfactory.

Reading activity 1

Note that in B Discussion, the students are presented with modal verbs as an input for the activity. Discuss their communicative meaning with the students, demonstrating with a key sentence, e.g. This motorway must/should/ought to/can, etc be completed by Christmas.

Writing activity 1

Give the students some examples to illustrate the differences given, e.g. Asking for advice as in the 'Dear Hester' letters (no immediate feedback)/Asking a friend for advice on the telephone (chance of immediate feedback).

Further possibilities for **a:** Writing – Capital letters = proper names, no intonation to give communicative meaning, etc. Speaking – no immediate evidence of proper names, intonation can enhance communicative meaning.

Reading activity 2

Ensure that students know about school exams. In England and Wales, at the age of 15 or 16, the more academic pupils in a school sit 'O' (Ordinary) levels. Some pupils remain at school until they are 18, when they can sit 'A' (Advanced) levels, usually in two or three subjects. These are academic, non-vocational exams, and university entrance usually depends on 'A' level grades. Less academic students can attend Further Education Colleges from the age of 16, where courses are more practical and where people already working can study part-time.
Note: changes will occur in this system over the next few years. This system does not apply in Scotland.

Key (A Analysis):
a A school student aged 15/16, academically better, intending to go to university.
b university entrance, wider range of careers, be able to understand basic principles and theory/analyse and comment on what you study.

Before doing B Discussion, ask about the situation in the students' own countries – what school examinations there are, what the problems are, what the advantages are, etc.

Listening activity 2

Key

a because she herself is elderly and she is a visitor of the elderly
b not enough food, exercise and money, careless with furniture
c that most of them live in long-stay hospitals
d Mrs Collins might have died
e visit the elderly regularly.

In discussion with the students, compare Mary Gerard's experiences and advice with situations in the students' own countries which are different from those described here.

Attitudes in Britain

Discuss with the class how prominently horoscopes feature in their own countries and establish the distinction between horoscopes found in specialist books and the day-to-day horoscopes found in newspapers. Point out the frequently vague or very general language used in horoscopes which can lead to varying interpretations, e.g. 'There may be difficulties at work'.

Unit Six

Listening activity 1

Here are your instructions:

One: Put the numbers 1 to 5 on every other line.
Two: Now write your name on line 4.
Three: Print the letters A–B–E–I–J–G on line 4, and circle the consonants.
Four: Listen carefully to the next instruction. Write your answer on line 2. If the 1914–18 War occurred before the turn of the century, write the larger of the numbers 16 and 20. If it did not, write 'cat'.
Five: Write your next answer on line 5. If A–P–P–L–E spells 'apple', and if 40 plus 10 makes 50, put an X. If not, draw a circle.

Listening activity 2

INTERVIEWER: On today's programme, *Education Now*, we have a special and unusual guest. Her name is Amalia Rodrigues and she is a teacher. More than full-time, because on Saturdays she runs a school for children of Latin American origin. Could you tell us, Amalia, why it was felt there was a need for a Saturday school?

AMALIA: There are many arguments about integration and bi-cultural education. And there is no one answer. But with other parents, I saw my children being brought up in British schools, learning British history. That, in itself, is a good thing. But not if the children can't read and write in their mother tongue or, perhaps, even speak it. Some of us are here for comparatively short periods of time; some are political refugees; some are immigrants. So, you see, we're quite a mixture. But the idea we all have in common is that our children should not forget their roots . . . and that they should be able to use their mother tongue. That they should not feel like strangers in the countries where their grandparents may still live.

INTERVIEWER: That seems a very good reason and I see the parents' point of view. How do the children feel about it? Is it just one more day of school with lessons in Spanish rather than English?

AMALIA: That's the way it began and, quite honestly, it was a failure. It wasn't what the children wanted so they wouldn't come. We were all teachers and we were determined to teach. The kids just wanted to have fun.

INTERVIEWER: So how has the school changed? Have the kids taken over?

AMALIA: If you're at all conventional, you might not call it a school in fact. Let me describe last Saturday. It took more than an hour for all the kids to arrive with their parents. Mind you, they range in age from 3 to 14. And they come from all over South London. Well, when we finally got started, we had parents in the kitchen preparing a Columbian meal for all of us. Upstairs, some teenagers were listening to Chilean folk music and tuning their own instruments. Downstairs, the 3 to 5-year-olds were learning a Mexican song. The 9-year-olds were having a Columbian day – learning about snakes and butterflies; trying on traditional clothes; drawing designs . . . all of this from a Columbian parent. Another group were preparing to exchange letters with a school in Nicaragua. Working quickly so that they could go out and play football. The borrowed minibus arrived to take 12 of the kids swimming. they wouldn't have the opportunity if we didn't take them . . . Am I talking too much?

INTERVIEWER: Not all all. I'm feeling rather envious: I had to go to school on Saturday, too, but we did Latin translation. One last question: Now that you've tasted failure and success, where do you see yourselves going from here?

AMALIA: We're still experimenting. And we're all very different. What we would like is a pilot school with a multi-cultural curriculum. We could take in children of all cultures and offer them an understanding of our common heritage. But that's a pipe dream . . . pie in the sky . . . castles in Spain, even. For the moment, we are happy to feel the energy and commitment from parents and children. And to provide a sort of Latin American street corner – a neighbourhood backyard.

INTERVIEWER: Thank you, Mrs Rodrigues, for being so open with us. We all wish you the best of luck in the future.

Notes

Introduction

Get students to describe awkward situations they have been in and how they dealt with them.

Listening activity 1

Relate the activity to the steps set out in the Introduction (above). The class will need to listen to the cassette several times before doing A Analysis.

Reading activity 1

Students should justify their explanations.

Writing activity

Students should be made aware of the necessity of producing more formal language than they have so far practised in this Unit for the writing activity.

Reading activity 2

Note that in B Discussion, the language chosen will differ depending on the channel of complaint used.

In the Roleplay it is important that the observer should remain impartial in the discussion and should report not only the details of the discussion but also whether s/he felt that the complainant was effective or not.

Listening activity 2

Key
a Fred's disappearance
b husband and wife

For the second part of the conversation the students should write down and add up all the numbers: 1927/51/42/37/32/64/13/20/57/93/92 = 2428. Get the students to speculate the reasons for this, e.g. Was Fred talking rubbish? Could he have been using a code? What significance might the message have? etc. The discussion should not be taken too seriously.

Attitudes in Britain

Cultural background: the main Budget is presented at the end of a financial year (end of March/beginning of April) and gives the Government's proposals for the raising and spending of public money for the forthcoming year. It has both political and economic content, e.g. lowering personal taxation just before an election (political) or lowering corporation tax to help industry/commerce (economic). The mini-budget is a statement by the Chancellor of the Exchequer (Economics Minister) halfway through the financial year showing any adjustments necessary.

Unit Seven

Listening activity 1
(MALE): I seem to be late. Couldn't be helped, I'm afraid. Traffic, you know. You've carried on, I see.
(CHILD): I didn't break your vase, Mummy. It just fell.

(FEMALE): I didn't know you'd forgotten your keys! You can hardly blame me for the fact that you had to walk home.
(MALE): Ahem. The unfortunate discrepancy in your account was the result of a computer error. I can assure you that immediate steps will be taken to return the account to a credit position.
(ANNOUNCER): Southern Rail regrets the late arrival of the 14.50 service from Brighton just arrived on platform 14. The delay was due to signal failure at Clapham Junction.
(MALE): What do you mean, 'illegally parked'? Show me the yellow line. Can't be illegal if there's no yellow line, can it?
(FEMALE): Oh, Vanessa, was it today? I have Friday in my diary. How silly of me. All I can say is that I'm sorry. Could we fix another date?

Listening activity 2
FRED: Hello. Hello . . . Is that you, Dee?
DEE: Hello. Hello. Daphne Weston here. Who's calling? Fred! Oh, Fred, I've been worrying for days. Where are you.
FRED: In a phone box. Didn't you notice? Now listen. If the police come round, tell them we're married.

DEE: But *we are* married!

FRED: Just make sure *they* know that. Wake up the kids. Get them to make a noise. Ha, ha! Shouldn't be difficult. You're always . . .

. . .

FRED: Are you there, Dee? Have you got a pencil and paper?

DEE: Have I what? Oh, a pencil. Hang on. Fred, why do I need a pencil?

FRED: Because you forget everything if you don't write it down.

. . .

DEE: Fred, are you there?

FRED: . . . Yes, I'm here. Now listen and do what I tell you. Write down *every* number I say; add them up and never mention this to anyone.

DEE: Look here, Fred, is this a comedy or a bad joke? It's 1.00 am and I haven't seen you since last week.

The children are upset and . . .

FRED: Daphne, this is important. Now, write. I was born in 1927. I lived at 51 42nd Street in the 37th precinct. My mother was 32 when I was born and my father was 64. A gap in age, you might say, but apparently my father was irresistible. Life was happy until I was 13, when my father went blind. It wasn't until I was 20 that I really understood and appreciated him. And not till now, at the age of 57, did I realise how much he meant to me. By the standards of his family, he died young. His mother remained well until the age of 93 and his father was buried at 92.

. . .

DEE: You're talking rubbish! Come home and relax. I can't cope with all this drama. Can't you explain?

FRED: Please, Dee. Do as I ask. I can't explain now.

. . .

Notes

Introduction

Note that the proverbs are contradictory: use them to illustrate that value judgements are made without understanding how they are made. Get the students to talk about proverbs in their own languages and give examples of other contradictory ones, e.g. many hands make light work/too many cooks spoil the broth.

Listening activity 1

A Analysis The objective is to demonstrate how ambiguous even simple instructions can be. The variation in the students' responses is caused by a lack of clarity in the instructions. Some of the reasons for this are:

– some of the instructions lack referents, e.g. 'Put the numbers 1–5 on every other line', does not make clear which line is the starting point.

– some are incomplete, e.g. 'Now write your name on line 4' does not make clear whether that is numbered line 4 or ruled line 4.

– some require different mental skills, e.g. instruction 5 requires spelling and mathematical skills.

– some require different types of answer, e.g. instruction 4 requires either 16, 20 or cat as an answer.

– the instructions are also not connected with one another. When receiving instructions, we expect there to be either a reasonably logical pattern to them or for a pattern to emerge.

Reading activity 1

Further practice Take a selection of magazine advertisements into class and get the students to describe, compare and comment on them.

Writing activity

Discuss the advertisement and vocabulary with the class, deciding who it is meant to appeal to, before doing the activity.

Reading activity 2

Discuss the photograph and map with the class to get their impressions before doing the activity.

Listening activity 2

The class should be given several opportunities to listen to this somewhat difficult interview. The first time they should listen for general comprehension, then listen and take notes and finally listen to complete the written activity. A discussion of bi-/multi-cultural education can take place after the written activity.

Attitudes in Britain

It may be necessary to introduce some vocabulary before the class does Analysis and Discussion **c** and **d**, e.g.: commuter, suburban, market town, pollution, etc.

Unit Eight

Listening activity 1

1

MALE: Claudia, what have you done with my car keys?

CLAUDIA: What have *I* done? Why accuse *me*?

MALE: You're always losing things, that's why.

CLAUDIA: And you're perfect, aren't you? Who flooded the bathroom yesterday? And last week, who burned the carpet? And what about the lamps you promised to replace, and . . .

MALE: Oh, shut up.

2

FEMALE: Now then, Miss Phillips. I've asked you to see me so that we can discuss your work performance. (Ahem) Why have you been such a failure in dealing with customers' complaints?

MISS PHILLIPS: What do you mean – a failure?

FEMALE: I have the figures in front of me. Eighty-two per cent of complaints referred to you have resulted in customers receiving rebates. It must be obvious that no business can be run that way.

MISS PHILLIPS: This isn't a business. It's dishonest trading.

3

FATHER: Charlie, I've been having a good look at your school report. It isn't good enough, you know. Non-achiever, they say. My son, a non-achiever. What have you got to say for yourself?

CHARLIE: Non-achiever? What does that mean?

FATHER: Speak up, Charles. Stop mumbling. Do you realise the sacrifices your mother and I have made to keep you at school? Don't you feel that you have a duty to succeed?

CHARLIE: Nobody ever asks me how *I* feel . . . what *I* want. I hate that school. I hate you, too. You're all bullies. You're fat and stupid, and you don't understand.

4

FEMALE: Tom, you're here at last. Overslept again, I suppose. Never mind. What's your excuse this time?

TOM: It isn't an excuse, exactly. What happened today was that my friend promised to pick me up and she never came so I had to walk and . . .

FEMALE: *She*, eh? Don't tell me you have a girlfriend? That explains it. Girlfriend or no girlfriend, see that it doesn't happen again. This is a business office, not a charity.

Listening activity 2

DAVID GREEN: Good morning. Good morning. Peter, Joe, Amy . . . the lot of you. It's 9.32. Time is money and this meeting is two minutes late in starting. In company terms, considering your salaries, that comes to about £5000. Even if you can afford it, the company can't. Ah . . . welcome hush. Miss Guest, please check those attending and read out any apologies.

MISS GUEST: Those present: Mr Green, Mrs Heatherington, Mr Flood, Mrs Gorbels, Miss Haver, Mr Tait. Apologies from Mr Tanimoto, Mrs Zweig, Monsieur Latour and Mr Umbale.

DAVID GREEN: Thank you, Miss Guest. Now, team . . . At the risk of boring you, I feel I must repeat the objectives of this meeting. Shall we dispense with the reading of the minutes? Right. Miss Guest, record minutes approved. Now to objectives: the keys are familiar to you – IP, RC, RPI.

CHORUS: Increase productivity . . . Reduce costs . . . Retain public image.

DAVID GREEN: Well done, team. Your loyalty is much appreciated. Now, the first point. Increase productivity. That's you, Joe Tait. We all know you're shy about speaking up.

JOE TAIT: We now have a scheme of offering very favourable mortgage rates for new key workers. A majority of these workers are happy to do overtime. A minority are union members. These facts should ensure stability of staff.

HELEN HEATHERINGTON: Joe, I must interrupt. Have they read and understood that 'favourable' rates are tied to their present jobs? Do they know they'll lose their investment if they change jobs?

PETER FLOOD: I'd like to hear about the sickness and absentee figures. Are they affected by overtime?

JOE TAIT: Consult the Occupational Health Department.
They are responsible for such details.

HELEN HEATHERINGTON: Why can't we have some straight answers?

DAVID GREEN: Thank you, Joe Tait. Now, Amy. Amy Gorbels. Tell us how you've reduced costs.

AMY GORBELS: A pleasure, and no problem. What we figured was that people here were getting too much for free. Like soap and towels. Okay, so there's a law. They have to wash their hands etcetera, we agree. But why our soap and towels? We talked with Sophie – Sophie Zweig. Her husband has a soap factory and we came up with the idea of giving every new employee a plastic bag with the company logo. We tell them that they can bring their own soap and towel in the bag. Or even better, buy them at the company store.

HELEN HEATHERINGTON: But that's illegal . . . and uncaring. Do you make these new employees pay to use the toilets?

AMY GORBELS: Good question. I was just going to talk about that. Too much work time is spent in toilets. We reckon we've saved the company 22 work hours overall by putting in pay toilets.

DAVID GREEN: Creative. Imaginative. Just what I like to hear, Amy. But time marches on and we have yet to hear from Edna Haver. Now, as you all know, Edna's on the verge of retirement so she has a special interest in pensions. Seriously, Edna, how are your social benefits going?

EDNA HAVER: Twenty per cent of our employees are seeking early retirement. They range in age from 50 for women and 57 for men. The pension position isn't very clear . . .

JOE TAIT: This emotional reaction is ridiculous. We are aware of our social responsibilities and . . .

HELEN HEATHERINGTON: Are we, Joe? I remember when you *were* aware. Edna, Edna Haver, may I say my piece first? Then we'd all like to hear from you.

DAVID GREEN: Mrs Heatherington, you're out of order, and you would be wise to control yourself.

HELEN HEATHERINGTON: Thank you, Mr Chairman. I have tried to raise several objections but somehow my voice has been ignored. May I first address my remarks to you. You, I believe, are 72. I am 35. Time is on my side. My husband and I own 52 per cent of the local British enterprise. You own 12 per cent. Money is on my side. And much more important, the workforce are on my side. I have here a petition signed by 90 per cent of the workforce, expressing their dissatisfaction with present conditions. They also demand a change of management. And so do I. This has become a matter of Them and Us. We have reached a point of confrontation.

EDNA HAVER: Thank you, Helen. I wouldn't have had the courage to say it, but it's what I've been wanting to . . .

DAVID GREEN: You're all out of order. This meeting is officially closed.

MISS GUEST: Excuse me, that's not possible. There hasn't been a vote. What am I to say in the Minutes?

PETER FLOOD: Don't worry, Miss Guest. Just say that the meeting adjourned on a note of disagreement.

Notes

Introduction

Discuss that, as the Introduction states, this is a consolidation unit and that students may wish to refer back to previous units as the need arises.

Listening activity 1

C Roleplay The students can either use the dialogues they have heard on cassette or they can make up dialogues based on the pictures of the confrontation situations. Refer back to Units 2 and 7 if necessary.

Reading activity 1

Refer back to Units 5 and 3 if necessary.

Writing activity

Remind the students of the various forms of a letter in English – business, personal, etc. Remind the students that the type of English used will depend on the recipient they choose. Get them to decide on what they are evaluating first and then to whom they are writing. Then let them write notes before attempting the complete letter.

Reading activity 2

Key
a Other fish in the sea, mistress, turn against, tawdry, depression.

b
Mother	A boy who the writer likes
Father	
A girl at the writer's school	An English teacher
	A Geography teacher

c Sunday dinner.
d Made her miserable and confused.
e Phyllis played Hamlet (a male) in the school play.
f Financial hardship caused by the depression.

B Roleplay and discussion It is important that the groups also report back to the whole class how the confrontations could have been avoided.

Listening activity 2

Key
a	6	b	£5000
c	time is money	d	the company
e	secretary	f	production/personnel manager

g by forcing a direct confrontation and by stating her control of the company's shares.